THE NOBLE WORDS

Remembrance and Prayers of

The Prophet Muḥammad

Shaykh-ul-Islam Ibn Taymiyah

(661-728 AH)

UK ISLAMIC ACADEMY

ISBN 1 872531 11 3

General Editor: Iqbal Ahmad Azami

Published by

UK Islamic Academy
PO Box 6645
Leicester LE5 5WT
United Kingdom

British Library Cataloguing in Publication Data

A catalogue record for this book is available from the British Library.

Contents

بِسْمِ اللهِ الرَّحْمَنِ الرَّحِيمِ

In the name of Allah, Most Gracious, Most Merciful

Foreword

THE NOBLE WORDS, Remembrance and Prayers of the Prophet Muḥammad ﷺ is a translation of *al-Kalim aṭ-Ṭayyib*, compiled by Shaykh-ul-Islam Abu'l-ʿAbbās Aḥmad Taqiyyu'd-Dīn ibn Taymiyah (661–728 AH, 1263–1328 CE). There are many books available on this subject in Arabic, some of which have been translated into English, but this book has its own special merits. Ibn Taymiyah is one of the greatest scholars of Islam, whose comments on certain subjects are regarded as final by most Muslim scholars. Imām Shamsu'd-Dīn adh-Dhahabī said that the authenticity of a *ḥadīth* approved by Ibn Taymiyah cannot be doubted.

This book has an extra blessing, in that it is an abridgement of *Kitāb al-Adhkār* of Imām Muḥyi'd-Dīn Abū Zakariyyā Yaḥyā ibn Sharaf an-Nawawī (631–676 AH, 1233–1276 CE), the celebrated commentator on Ṣaḥīḥ Muslim and a great scholar of Islamic learning. His book *Kitāb al-Adhkār* is known as the best collection on the subject of remembrance of Allah and prayers, according to the way of the Prophet Muḥammad, may Allah bless him and grant him peace, his Companions and the people who followed them with sincerity and devotion.

This book also has another merit, in that it was published in Arabic by al-Maktab al-Islami of Damascus and Beirut, with editing and research by one of the greatest scholars of *ḥadīth* in the contemporary world, Shaykh Nāṣir ad-Dīn al-Albānī, may Allah have mercy on him and reward him for his service to the *Sunnah*.

It is appropriate at this point to clarify that this collection includes some *aḥādīth* with weak *isnād*, which have usually been accepted by the Imāms of the science of *ḥadīth* for these kinds of subjects, though they are more strict about the narrations concerning legal matters.

Imām Ibn Taymiyah and Imām an-Nawawī, may Allah have mercy on them both, have included these *aḥādīth* in their books,

5

proof that they were of the opinion that one should accept *aḥādīth* on these kinds of subjects, even with *isnāds* which have some technical weaknesses according to the science of *ḥadīth*. Ibn Taymiyah has also included in this collection practices of some of the Companions, and some of his personal experiences to give a wider understanding of this matter. We have included in the translation the comments of the author himself on the technical position of the *aḥādīth* and also some of Shaykh al-Albānī's comments from the footnotes of his original Arabic edition.

Allah, exalted is He, knows all the languages of His creatures. A person can remember Him and pray to Him in any language or with any expression. But, undoubtedly, the way of remembrance and the blessed words of the Prophet, may Allah bless him and grant him peace, with which he prayed to Allah, are more likely to be answered. Therefore, we have included in this book the noble words of remembrance of Allah and the prayers in Arabic with their Arabic vowel markings, and their translations in English. It is, of course, preferable to supplicate in Arabic, thereby completely understanding the meaning.

We hope this book will be useful for remembering Allah, glorious and exalted is He, and for supplicating to Him for all the needs of life, with confidence and understanding.

I am grateful to my daughter Suʿād, for her great contribution in preparing the translation, may Allah reward her for this noble effort, and give her *tawfīq* in following the *Sunnah* of the Prophet, the blessings and peace of Allah be upon him, and in moulding her life according to his blessed way. I am also grateful to Dr M.M. Ahsan and Br Mokrane for reading a substantial part of the book and suggesting some improvements and Br Abdassamad Clarke for editing.

May Allah bless them all for their noble efforts in this cause, and make it of use in the service of Allah. To Allah belongs all good, and by His favours all righteous deeds come into existence.

Leicester, United kingdom   **Iqbal Ahmad Azami**
Rabīʿ al-Awwal 1424 AH

In the name of Allah, the Most Beneficent, the Most Merciful
O Allah, bless the noblest of Your creatures Muhammad. To Allah alone belongs all praise and He suffices, and peace be upon His slaves whom He chooses. I testify that there is no god but Allah alone without partner, and I testify that Muhammad ﷺ is His slave and Messenger.

Allah, exalted is He, says:

يَا أَيُّهَا الَّذِينَ آمَنُوا اتَّقُوا اللَّهَ وَقُولُوا قَوْلاً سَدِيدًا يُصْلِحْ لَكُمْ أَعْمَالَكُمْ وَيَغْفِرْ لَكُمْ ذُنُوبَكُمْ

"O you who believe, guard your duty to Allah and speak words straight to the point; He will adjust your works for you and will forgive you your wrong actions."
(Qur'an, al-Ahzab: 70-71)

And He, exalted is He, says:

إِلَيْهِ يَصْعَدُ الْكَلِمُ الطَّيِّبُ وَالْعَمَلُ الصَّالِحُ يَرْفَعُهُ

"To Him good words ascend, and the right action He exalts."
(Qur'an, al-Fatir: 10)

And He, exalted is He, says:

فَاذْكُرُونِي أَذْكُرْكُمْ وَاشْكُرُوا لِي

"Therefore remember Me, I will remember you, and give thanks to Me..."
(Qur'an, al-Baqarah: 152)

And He, exalted is He, says:

اذْكُرُوا اللَّهَ ذِكْرًا كَثِيرًا

"Remember Allah, with much remembrance."

(Qur'an, al-Ahzab: 41)

And He, exalted is He, says:

وَالذَّاكِرِينَ اللَّهَ كَثِيرًا وَالذَّاكِرَات

"...and men who remember Allah much and women who remember...."

(Qur'an, al-Ahzab: 35)

And He, exalted is He, says:

الَّذِينَ يَذْكُرُونَ اللَّهَ قِيَامًا وَقُعُودًا وَعَلَى جُنُوبِهِمْ

"...such as remember Allah, standing, sitting and reclining"

(Qur'an, Al ʿImran: 191)

And He, exalted is He, says:

إِذَا لَقِيتُمْ فِئَةً فَاثْبُتُوا وَاذْكُرُوا اللَّهَ كَثِيرًا

"When you meet an army, hold firm and remember Allah much."

(Qur'an, al-Anfal: 45)

And He, exalted is He, says:

فَإِذَا قَضَيْتُمْ مَنَاسِكَكُمْ فَاذْكُرُوا اللَّهَ كَذِكْرِكُمْ آبَاءَكُمْ أَوْ أَشَدَّ ذِكْرًا

"And when you have completed your devotions, then remember Allah as you remember your fathers or with a more lively remembrance."

(Qur'an, al-Baqarah: 200)

And He, exalted is He, says:

لاَ تُلْهِكُمْ أَمْوَالُكُمْ وَلاَ أَوْلاَدُكُمْ عَنْ ذِكْرِ اللَّهِ

"Let not your wealth nor your children distract you from remembrance of Allah."

(Qur'an, al-Munafiqun: 9)

And He, exalted is He, says:

رِجَالٌ لاَ تُلْهِيهِمْ تِجَارَةٌ وَلاَ بَيْعٌ عَنْ ذِكْرِ اللَّهِ وَإِقَامِ الصَّلَاةِ وَإِيتَاءِ الزَّكَاةِ

"...men whom neither trade nor purchase distract from the remembrance of Allah and the establishment of the prayer and the production of the zakah."

(Qur'an, an-Nur: 37)

And He, exalted is He, says:

وَاذْكُرْ رَبَّكَ فِي نَفْسِكَ تَضَرُّعًا وَخِيفَةً وَدُونَ الْجَهْرِ مِنَ الْقَوْلِ بِالْغُدُوِّ وَالآصَالِ وَلاَ تَكُنْ مِنَ الْغَافِلِينَ

"And remember your Lord within yourself humbly and with awe, below your breath at morn and evening. And be not of the neglectful."

(Qur'an, al-A'raf: 205)

1. On the virtues of *dhikr*

1. Abu ad-Darda' ٱللّٰهُ said: Allah's Messenger ﷺ said, "Shall I tell you the best and purest of your deeds in the estimation of your Master, those which are the highest in degrees, those which are better for you than spending gold and silver, and are better for you than that you should meet your enemy and cut off one another's heads?" They said, "Yes, Messenger of Allah." He said, "It is the remembrance of Allah." (At-Tirmidhi and Ibn Majah transmitted this *hadith* and al-Hakim commented, "It's *isnad* is sound.")

2. Abu Hurairah ٱللّٰهُ said: Allah's Messenger ﷺ said, "The *mufarridun* have gone ahead and excelled." They asked, "Who are the *mufarridun*, Messenger of Allah?" He replied, "Those men and women who remember Allah much." (Muslim)

3. ʿAbdullah ibn Busr ٱللّٰهُ mentioned that a man said, "O Messenger of Allah! the ordinances of *iman* have become too many for me, so tell me something to which I can cling." He replied, "Let your tongue not cease to be moist with the remembrance of Allah, exalted is He." (At-Tirmidhi transmitted it, saying, "This is a *hasan hadith*.")

4. Abu Musa al-Ashʿari ٱللّٰهُ reported the Prophet ﷺ as saying, "The examples of one who remembers his Lord and one who does not are like the living and the dead." (Bukhari)

5. Abu Hurairah ٱللّٰهُ reported Allah's Messenger ﷺ as saying, "If one sits in a place where he does not remember Allah, exalted is He, there will be deprivation for him from Allah; and if one lies down in a place where he does not remember Allah, exalted is He, there will be deprivation for him from Allah." (Abu Dawud)

2. On the virtues of *tasbih, tahlil, tahmid,* and *takbir*

6. Abu Hurairah ؓ reported Allah's Messenger ﷺ as saying, "Whoever says a hundred times in a day:

لاَ إِلَهَ إِلاَّ اللَّهُ وَحْدَهُ لاَ شَرِيكَ لَهُ ، لَهُ الْمُلْكُ ، وَلَهُ الْحَمْدُ ،
وَهُوَ عَلَى كُلِّ شَيْءٍ قَدِيرٌ "

'There is no god but Allah alone without partner; His is the dominion, and His the praise, and He is able to do all things,'
will have a reward equivalent to that of freeing ten slaves, a hundred rewards recorded for him, a hundred sins obliterated [from his record]; and it will be a protection for him from Shaytan all that day till evening; and no one will excel him, except a man who has done more than he has." (Bukhari, Muslim)

7. And [Abu Hurairah ؓ also reported that Allah's Messenger ﷺ] said, "If anyone says a hundred times in a day:

سُبْحَانَ اللَّهِ وَبِحَمْدِهِ

'Glory be to Allah, and [I begin] with praise of Him,' ~~Excellent~~
his wrong actions will be removed from him even if they were like the foam of the sea." (Bukhari, Muslim)

8. Abu Hurairah ؓ said: Allah's Messenger ﷺ said, "Two expressions, [which are] light on the tongue, heavy in the scale and dear to the Compassionate One, are:

سُبْحَانَ اللَّهِ وَبِحَمْدِهِ سُبْحَانَ اللَّهِ الْعَظِيمِ

✳ *'Glory be to Allah, and [I begin] with praise of Him; and Glory be to Allah the Incomparably Great'.*" (Bukhari, Muslim)

9. Abu Hurairah ؓ said: Allah's Messenger ﷺ said, "To say:

سُبْحَانَ اللَّهِ ، وَالْحَمْدُ لِلَّهِ ، وَلاَ إِلَهَ إِلاَّ اللَّهُ ، وَاللَّهُ أَكْبَرُ

* 'Glory be to Allah; Praise be to Allah; there is no god but Allah;
   and Allah is most great,'

is dearer to me than everything over which the sun rises." (Muslim)

10. Samurah ibn Jundub ﷺ said: Allah's Messenger ﷺ said,
"The words dearest to Allah are four. It does not matter which
you say first:

سُبْحَانَ اللَّهِ ، وَالْحَمْدُ لِلَّهِ ، وَلاَ إِلَهَ إِلاَّ اللَّهُ ، وَاللَّهُ أَكْبَرُ

'Glory be to Allah; Praise be to Allah; there is no god but Allah;
and Allah is most great,'" (Muslim)

11. Sa'd ibn Abi Waqqas ﷺ said: Once we were with Allah's
Messenger ﷺ and he asked, "Are any of you incapable of
acquiring a thousand rewards daily?" One of those who were
sitting with him asked, "How can any of us acquire a thousand
rewards?" He replied, "If he glorifies [Allah] a hundred times, a
thousand rewards will be recorded for him or a thousand wrong
actions will be removed from him." (Muslim)

12. Juwairiyah, the mother of the believers ﷺ said that the Prophet
ﷺ went out after morning prayer leaving her sitting in her
place of prayer (making dhikr and du'a). He returned in the forenoon
and she was still sitting [in the same place]. He asked, "Have you
continued in the same position I left you in?" She said, "Yes." So
the Prophet ﷺ said, "Since leaving you I have said four phrases
three times which, if weighed against all you have said today,
would prove to be heavier:

سُبْحَانَ اللَّهِ عَدَدَ خَلْقِهِ ، سُبْحَانَ اللَّهِ رِضَى نَفْسِهِ ،
سُبْحَانَ اللَّهِ زِنَةَ عَرْشِهِ ، سُبْحَانَ اللَّهِ مِدَادَ كَلِمَاتِهِ

* 'Glory be to Allah, as much as the number of His creatures;

glory be to Allah, in accordance with His good pleasure; glory be to Allah, to the weight of His throne; glory be to Allah to the extent of His words (lit: according to the ink of His words).'" (Muslim)

13. Sa'd ibn Abi Waqqas ؓ said that along with the Prophet ﷺ he once visited a woman in front of whom were some date-stones or pebbles which she was using [to keep count] in glorifying Allah. The Prophet ﷺ said, "Shall I not tell you something which would be easier (or better) for you than that? [and he told her it consisted of saying]:

سُبْحَانَ اللَّهِ عَدَدَ مَا خَلَقَ فِي السَّمَاءِ ، وَسُبْحَانَ اللَّهِ عَدَدَ مَا خَلَقَ فِي الأَرْضِ ، وَسُبْحَانَ اللَّهِ عَدَدَ مَا بَيْنَ ذَٰلِكَ ، وَسُبْحَانَ اللَّهِ عَدَدَ مَا هُوَ خَالِقٌ ، وَاللَّهُ أَكْبَرُ مِثْلُ ذَٰلِكَ ، وَالْحَمْدُ لِلَّهِ مِثْلُ ذَٰلِكَ ، وَلاَ إِلَهَ إِلاَّ اللَّهُ مِثْلُ ذَٰلِكَ ، وَلاَ حَوْلَ وَلاَ قُوَّةَ إِلاَّ بِاللَّهِ مِثْلُ ذَٰلِكَ

'Glory be to Allah as many times as the number of what He has created in the heaven; Glory be to Allah as many times as the number of what He has created in the earth; Glory be to Allah as many times as the number of what is between them; Glory be to Allah as many times as the number of what He will create; Allah is most great, a similar number of times; Praise be to Allah, a similar number of times; There is no god but Allah, a similar number of times; There is no might and no power except in Allah, a similar number of times.'" (At-Tirmidhi, Abu Dawud. At-Tirmidhi said, "This is a *hasan hadith*.")

14. Sa'd ibn Abi Waqqas ؓ said that a bedouin came to the Prophet ﷺ and said, "Messenger of Allah teach me some words to say." He told him to say:

لاَ إِلَهَ إِلاَّ اللَّهُ وَحْدَهُ لاَ شَرِيكَ لَهُ ، اللَّهُ أَكْبَرُ كَبِيرًا ،

وَالْحَمْدُ لِلَّهِ كَثِيرًا ، وَسُبْحَانَ اللَّهِ رَبِّ الْعَالَمِينَ ، وَلاَ
حَوْلَ وَلاَ قُوَّةَ إِلاَّ بِاللَّهِ الْعَزِيزِ الْحَكِيمِ

*'There is no god but Allah alone who has no partner; Allah is
very great; Abundant praise is due to Allah; Glory be to Allah,
the Lord of the universe; There is no might and no power except
in Allah, the Mighty, the Wise.'"*

He remarked, "These are for my Lord but what should I say for
myself?" He told him to say:

اَللَّهُمَّ اغْفِرْ لِي ، وَارْحَمْنِي ، وَاهْدِنِي ، وَعَافِنِي ، وَارْزُقْنِي

*'O Allah, forgive me, show mercy to me, guide me, grant me
well-being and provide for me.'"*

When the bedouin left, the Prophet ﷺ commented, "The man
filled both his hands with good." (Muslim)

15. Ibn Mas'ud ؓ said: Allah's Messenger ﷺ said, "I met
Ibrahim on the night I was taken up to heaven, and he said, 'O
Muhammad! convey my greeting to your people, and tell them
that Paradise has good soil and sweet water, it consists of level,
treeless plains, and its plants are:

سُبْحَانَ اللَّهِ ، وَالْحَمْدُ لِلَّهِ ، وَلاَ إِلَهَ إِلاَّ اللَّهُ ، وَاللَّهُ أَكْبَرُ

٭ *"Glory be to Allah; Praise be to Allah; There is no god but Allah;
and Allah is most great".'"* (At-Tirmidhi said, "A *hasan hadith*.")

16. Abu Musa al-Ash'ari ؓ said: The Prophet ﷺ said to me,
"Would you like me to guide you to one of the treasures of the
Garden?" I said, "Certainly, Messenger of Allah." He said, "Say:

لاَحَوْلَ وَلاَ قُوَّةَ إِلاَّ بِاللَّهِ

٭ *'There is no might and no power except by Allah.'"* (Bukhari,
Muslim)

14

3. Virtue of remembering Allah morning and evening

Allah, exalted is He, says:

$$يَاأَيُّهَا الَّذِينَ آمَنُوا اذْكُرُوا اللَّهَ ذِكْرًا كَثِيرًا وَسَبِّحُوهُ بُكْرَةً وَأَصِيلاً$$

"O you who believe remember Allah with much remembrance and glorify Him morning and evening."

(Qur'an, al-Ahzab: 41)

And He, exalted is He, says:

$$وَاذْكُرْ رَبَّكَ فِي نَفْسِكَ تَضَرُّعًا وَخِيفَةً وَدُونَ الْجَهْرِ مِنَ الْقَوْلِ بِالْغُدُوِّ وَالآصَالِ وَلاَ تَكُنْ مِنَ الْغَافِلِينَ$$

"And remember your Lord within yourself humbly and with awe, below your breath at morn and evening. And be not of the neglectful."

(Qur'an, al-A'raf: 205)

And He, exalted is He, says:

$$وَسَبِّحْ بِحَمْدِ رَبِّكَ بِالْعَشِيِّ وَالإِبْكَارِ$$

"And hymn the praise of your Lord at fall of night and in the early hours."

(Qur'an, Ghafir: 55)

And He, exalted is He, says:

$$وَسَبِّحْ بِحَمْدِ رَبِّكَ قَبْلَ طُلُوعِ الشَّمْسِ وَقَبْلَ الْغُرُوبِ$$

"And hymn the praise of your Lord before the rising and before the setting [of the sun]."

(Qur'an, Qaf: 39)

And He, exalted is He, says:

وَلاَ تَطْرُدِ الَّذِينَ يَدْعُونَ رَبَّهُمْ بِالْغَدَاةِ وَالْعَشِيِّ يُرِيدُونَ وَجْهَهُ

"Repel not those who call upon their Lord at morn and evening, seeking His countenance."
(Qur'an, al-An'am: 52)

فَأَوْحَى إِلَيْهِمْ أَنْ سَبِّحُوا بُكْرَةً وَعَشِيّاً

"And he [Zakariyya] signified to them, 'Glorify [your Lord] at break of day and fall of night.'"
(Qur'an, Maryam: 11)

وَمِنَ اللَّيْلِ فَسَبِّحْهُ وَإِدْبَارَ النُّجُومِ

"And in the night-time also glorify Him, and at the setting of the stars."
(Qur'an, at-Tur: 49)

فَسُبْحَانَ اللَّهِ حِينَ تُمْسُونَ وَحِينَ تُصْبِحُونَ

"So glory be to Allah when you enter the night and when you enter the morning."
(Qur'an, ar-Rum: 17)

وَأَقِمِ الصَّلاَةَ طَرَفَيِ النَّهَارِ وَزُلَفًا مِنَ اللَّيْلِ إِنَّ الْحَسَنَاتِ يُذْهِبْنَ السَّيِّئَاتِ

"Establish the prayer at the two ends of the day and in some watches of the night. Truly, good deeds annul ill deeds."
(Qur'an, Hud: 114)

17. Abu Hurairah ؓ said: The Prophet ﷺ said, "Whoever

16

says a hundred times morning and evening:

$$\text{سُبْحَانَ اللَّه وَبِحَمْدِه}$$

'Glory be to Allah, and [I begin] with praise of Him,'
only one who said what he said, or more than it, will bring anything
more excellent than him on the day of resurrection." (Muslim)

18. ʿAbdullah ibn Masʿud ﷺ said that "When evening came the
Prophet of Allah ﷺ would say:

$$\text{أَمْسَيْنَا وَأَمْسَى الْمُلْكُ للَّه ، وَالْحَمْدُ للَّه ، لاَ إِلَهَ إِلاَّ اللَّهُ}$$
$$\text{وَحْدَهُ لاَ شَرِيكَ لَهُ ، لَهُ الْمُلْكُ وَلَهُ الْحَمْدُ ، وَهُوَ عَلَى كُلِّ}$$
$$\text{شَيْءٍ قَدِيرٌ ، رَبِّ أَسْأَلُكَ خَيْرَ مَا فِي هذه اللَّيْلَة ، وَخَيْرَ}$$
$$\text{مَا بَعْدَهَا ، وَأَعُوذُ بِكَ مِنْ شَرِّ مَا فِي هذه اللَّيْلَة ، وَشَرِّ مَا}$$
$$\text{بَعْدَهَا ، رَبِّ أَعُوذُ بِكَ مِنَ الْكَسَلِ ، وَسُوءِ الْكِبَرِ ، رَبِّ}$$
$$\text{أَعُوذُ بِكَ مِنْ عَذَابٍ فِي النَّارِ ، وَعَذَابٍ فِي الْقَبْرِ}$$

*'We have come to the evening, and the dominion belongs to
Allah; praise be to Allah; there is no god but Allah alone without
any partner; to Him belongs dominion, to Him praise is due,
and He is omnipotent. O Lord, I ask You for the good of this
night, and the good of what it contains and for the good that
follows it, and I seek refuge with You from the mischief of this
night and the mischief of what it contains and from the mischief
that follows it. O my Lord, I seek refuge with You from laziness
and the difficulties of old age. My Lord, I seek refuge with You
from a punishment in the Fire and a punishment in the grave."*
In the morning he said that also [but began instead with]:

$$\text{أَصْبَحْنَا وَأَصْبَحَ الْمُلْكُ للَّه}$$

*"We have come to the morning and the dominion belongs to
Allah."* (Muslim)

19. ʿAbdullah ibn Khubayb ؓ said: We went out one rainy and intensely dark night to look for Allah's Messenger ﷺ that he might pray for us, and when we caught up with him, he said, "Speak (*Qul*)!" I kept quiet, then he said, "Speak." [But] I did not say anything, then he [once again] said, "Speak." I asked him, "What should I say, Messenger of Allah?" He replied, "*Qul Huwa'llahu Ahad* and *al-Muʿawwidhatain* three times morning and evening, will suffice you for every purpose (protect you from every mischief)." (Abu Dawud, an-Nasa'i, at-Tirmidhi. At-Tirmidhi said, "A *hasan sahih hadith*.")

20. Abu Hurairah ؓ mentioned that Allah's Messenger ﷺ used to teach his Companions, saying, "When any of you gets up in the morning let him say:

اَللّٰهُمَّ بِكَ أَصْبَحْنَا ، وَبِكَ أَمْسَيْنَا ، وَبِكَ نَحْيَا ، وَبِكَ نَمُوتُ ، وَإِلَيْكَ النُّشُورُ

'O Allah! By You we come to the morning, by You we come to the evening, by You we live, by You we die, and to You will be the resurrection,'
and in the evening let him say:

اَللّٰهُمَّ بِكَ أَمْسَيْنَا ، وَبِكَ أَصْبَحْنَا ، وَبِكَ نَحْيَا ، وَبِكَ نَمُوتُ ، وَإِلَيْكَ الْمَصِيرُ

'O Allah! By You we come to the evening, by You we come to the morning, by You we live, by You we die, and to You is the return."
(At-Tirmidhi transmitted it, saying, "This is a *hasan sahih hadith*.")

21. Shaddad ibn Aws ؓ reported Allah's Messenger ﷺ as saying, "The best way of asking forgiveness is to say:

اَللّٰهُمَّ أَنْتَ رَبِّي ، لَا إِلَهَ إِلَّا أَنْتَ ، خَلَقْتَنِي وَأَنَا عَبْدُكَ ، وَأَنَا عَلَى عَهْدِكَ وَوَعْدِكَ مَا اسْتَطَعْتُ ، أَعُوذُ بِكَ مِنْ شَرِّ

$$\text{مَـا صَنَعْتُ، أَبُوءُ لَكَ بِنِعْمَـتِكَ عَلَيَّ، وَأَبُوءُ بِذَنْبِي،}$$

$$\text{فَاغْفِرْلِي، فَإِنَّهُ لاَ يَغْفِرُ الذُّنُوبَ إِلاَّ أَنْتَ}$$

'O Allah, You are my Lord. There is no god but You. You have created me, and I am Your slave and hold to Your covenant and promise as much as I can. I seek refuge in You from the mischief of what I have done. I acknowledge Your favour to me, and I acknowledge my wrong action, so pardon me, for none pardons wrong actions but You.'

Whoever says it during the night and dies before morning will enter the Garden and whoever says it during the morning and dies that day before evening will enter the Garden." (Bukhari)

22. Abu Hurairah ؓ reported that Abu Bakr as-Siddiq ؓ said, "Messenger of Allah! Teach me something to say in the morning and the evening." He said, "Say:

$$\text{اَللّهُمَّ عَالِمَ الْغَيْبِ وَالشَّهَادَة، فَاطِرَ السَّمَـوَاتِ وَالأَرْضِ،}$$

$$\text{رَبَّ كُلِّ شَيْءٍ وَمَلِيكَهُ، أَشْـهَدُ أَنْ لاَ إِلَهَ إِلاَّ أَنْتَ، أَعُوذُ بِكَ}$$

$$\text{مِنْ شَرِّ نَفْسِي، وَشَرِّ الشَّيْطَانِ وَشِرْكِه}$$

'O Allah, Knower of the unseen and the seen, Creator of the heavens and the earth, Lord and Possessor of everything, I testify that there is no god but You; I seek refuge with You from the mischief of myself, from the mischief of the Shaytan and his [incitement to] attributing partners [to Allah],'

And in another version:

$$\text{وَأَنْ أَقْتَرِفَ عَلَى نَفْسِي سُوءًا أَوْ أَجُرَّهُ إِلَى مُسْلِمٍ}$$

'And [I seek refuge with You] that I should commit against my own self a mischief or bring it upon a Muslim,'

Say it morning and evening, and when you go to bed." (At-Tirmidhi transmitted it, saying, "A *hasan sahih hadith*.")

23. ʿUthman ibn ʿAffan ﷺ said: Allah's Messenger ﷺ said, "If any slave [of Allah] says upon the morning of every day and on the evening of every night:

بِسْمِ اللّٰهِ الَّذِي لَا يَضُرُّ مَعَ اسْمِهِ شَيْءٌ فِي الْأَرْضِ وَلَا فِي السَّمَاءِ ، وَهُوَ السَّمِيعُ الْعَلِيمُ

'In the name of Allah, the One along with whose name nothing in earth or heaven can cause harm, and He is the Hearer, the Knower,'

three times, he will not be harmed by anything." (At-Tirmidhi transmitted it, saying, "This is a *hasan sahih hadith*.")

24. Thawban ﷺ and others, reported Allah's Messenger ﷺ as saying, "Whoever says in the evening:

رَضِيتُ بِاللّٰهِ رَبًّا ، وَبِالْإِسْلَامِ دِينًا ، وَبِمُحَمَّدٍ صَلَّى اللّٰهُ عَلَيْهِ وَسَلَّمَ نَبِيًّا

'I am pleased with Allah as Lord, with Islam as a way of life, and with Muhammad ﷺ as Prophet,'

then Allah must please him." (At-Tirmidhi transmitted it, saying, "This is a *hasan sahih hadith*.")

25. Anas ﷺ reported Allah's Messenger ﷺ as saying, "If anyone says in the morning or evening:

اَللّٰهُمَّ إِنِّي أَصْبَحْتُ أُشْهِدُكَ ، وَأُشْهِدُ حَمَلَةَ عَرْشِكَ ، وَمَلَائِكَتَكَ ، وَجَمِيعَ خَلْقِكَ بِأَنَّكَ أَنْتَ اللّٰهُ لَا إِلَهَ إِلَّا أَنْتَ ، وَأَنَّ مُحَمَّدًا عَبْدُكَ وَرَسُولُكَ

'O Allah, I call You to witness, and I call the bearers of Your Throne, Your angels and all Your creatures to witness that You are Allah [and] there is no god except You, and that Muhammad is Your slave and Messenger,'

Then Allah will free a quarter of him from the Fire. Whoever says it twice, Allah will free half of him from the Fire. Whoever says it three times, Allah will free three-quarters of him from the Fire. Whoever says it four times, Allah will free him from the Fire [completely]." (At-Tirmidhi transmitted it, saying, "This is a *hasan hadith*.")

26. ʿAbdullah ibn Ghannam reported Allah's Messenger as saying, "If anyone says in the morning:

اَللَّهُمَّ مَا أَصْبَحَ بِي مِنْ نِعْمَةٍ [أَوْ بِأَحَدٍ مِنْ خَلْقِكَ] فَمِنْكَ وَحْدَكَ لاَشَرِيكَ لَكَ ، لَكَ الْحَمْدُ ، وَلَكَ الشُّكْرُ

'O Allah, whatever favour has come to me [or to any of Your creatures], then [it comes] from You alone who have no partner, to You be praise and to You be thanks,'

then he will have expressed full thanks for the day; and if anyone says the same in the evening he will have expressed full thanks for the night." (Abu Dawud)

27. ʿAbdullah ibn ʿUmar said: Allah's Messenger never failed to use these words in the evening and morning:

اَللَّهُمَّ إِنِّي أَسْأَلُكَ الْعَافِيَةَ فِي الدُّنْيَا وَالآخِرَةِ ، اَللَّهُمَّ أَسْأَلُكَ الْعَفْوَ وَالْعَافِيَةَ فِي دِينِي وَدُنْيَايَ ، وَأَهْلِي وَمَالِي ، اَللَّهُمَّ اسْتُرْ عَوْرَاتِي ، وَآمِنْ رَوْعَاتِي ، اَللَّهُمَّ احْفَظْنِي مِنْ بَيْنِ يَدَيَّ وَمِنْ خَلْفِي ، وَعَنْ يَمِينِي وَعَنْ شِمَالِي ، وَمِنْ فَوْقِي ، وَأَعُوذُ بِعَظَمَتِكَ أَنْ أُغْتَالَ مِنْ تَحْتِي

"O Allah, I ask You for well-being in this world and the next; O Allah, I ask You for pardon and well-being in my religion and my worldly affairs, in my family and my property; O Allah, conceal my faults and keep me safe from the things which I fear;

＊ *O Allah, guard me [from all evils] from in front or behind, from my right or from my left, and from above me; and I seek refuge in Your greatness from receiving unexpected harm from below me."*

Waki' said, "He meant [by the latter] being swallowed up by the earth." (Abu Dawud, an-Nasa'i and Ibn Majah. Al-Hakim commented, "Its *isnad* is *sahih*.")

28. Talq ibn Habib said: A man came to Abu ad-Darda' ؓ and said, "Abu ad-Darda', your house has burnt down." He responded, "It has not burnt down. Allah would not let it happen so, because of some words about which I heard the Messenger of Allah ﷺ saying that whoever says them at the beginning of the day, then no affliction will reach him until the evening, and whoever says them at the end of the day, then no affliction will reach him until the morning. [Those words are]:

اَللَّهُمَّ أَنْتَ رَبِّي لاَ إِلَهَ إِلاَّ أَنْتَ ، عَلَيْكَ تَوَكَّلْتُ ، وَأَنْتَ رَبُّ الْعَرْشِ الْعَظِيمِ ، مَا شَاءَ اللَّهُ كَانَ ، وَمَا لَمْ يَشَأْ لَمْ يَكُنْ ، لاَ حَوْلَ وَلاَ قُوَّةَ إِلاَّ بِاللَّهِ الْعَلِيِّ الْعَظِيمِ ، أَعْلَمُ أَنَّ اللَّهَ عَلَى كُلِّ شَيْءٍ قَدِيرٌ ، وَأَنَّ اللَّهَ قَدْ أَحَاطَ بِكُلِّ شَيْءٍ عِلْمًا ، اَللَّهُمَّ إِنِّي أَعُوذُ بِكَ مِنْ شَرِّ نَفْسِي ، وَمِنْ شَرِّ كُلِّ دَابَّةٍ أَنْتَ آخِذٌ بِنَاصِيَتِهَا ، إِنَّ رَبِّي عَلَى صِرَاطٍ مُسْتَقِيمٍ

＊ *'O Allah, You are my Lord, there is no god but You, in You I place my trust; You are the Lord of the magnificent Throne; whatever Allah wills occurs, and whatever He does not wish to be does not occur; there is no might and no power except by Allah, the High and Great. I know that Allah has power over everything and Allah encompasses everything with His knowledge. O Allah, I seek refuge in You from the mischief of myself, and from the mischief of every animal on the earth whose forehead you hold; surely the straight path is with my Lord.'"*[1]

---

[1] A weak *hadith*; Ibn as-Sunni transmitted it.

4. What should be said at bed-time

29. Hudhaifah رضي الله عنه said: When the Messenger of Allah ﷺ intended to sleep, he would say:

بِاسْمِكَ اللَّهُمَّ أَمُوتُ وَأَحْيَا

✳ *"In Your name, O Allah, I die and live."*

When he awoke he would say:

الْحَمْدُ لِلَّهِ الَّذِي أَحْيَانَا بَعْدَ مَا أَمَاتَنَا وَإِلَيْهِ النُّشُورُ

✳ *'Praise be to Allah who has given us life after causing us to die, and to Whom is the resurrection.'"* (Bukhari, Muslim)

30. ᶜA'ishah رضي الله عنها said: Every night when the Prophet ﷺ went to his bed he joined his hands and breathed into them, reciting into them, *Surah Qul Huwa'llahu Ahad*; *Surah Qul Aᶜudhu Bi Rabbi'l-Falaq*; and *Surah Qul Aᶜudhu Bi Rabbi'n-nas*. Then he would wipe as much of his body as he could with them [his hands], beginning with his head, his face and the front of his body, doing that three times. (Bukhari, Muslim)

31. Abu Hurairah رضي الله عنه related that someone came to him night after night, and the Prophet ﷺ had placed him in charge of the *zakah*. When it happened on the third night, he seized him and said, "I am certainly going to take you before Allah's Messenger ﷺ." He said, "If you let me go I will teach you some words by which Allah will benefit you" – and they [the Companions] were very keen to learn good things. He said, "When you go to your bed recite *Ayat al-Kursi*, to the end of the *ayah*, for a guardian from Allah will then remain over you and no Shaytan will come near you till the morning." [Hearing the story the Prophet ﷺ] said, "He has certainly told you the truth though he is a great liar. That was a shaytan." (Bukhari)

32. Abu Masᶜud ﷺ reported Allah's Messenger ﷺ as saying, "If anyone recites the two *ayahs* at the end of Surah al-Baqarah at night they will suffice him." (Bukhari, Muslim)

33. ᶜAli ﷺ said, "I do not consider that anyone with intelligence would sleep before reading three *ayat* from the end of Surah al-Baqarah."

34. Abu Hurairah ﷺ reported Allah's Messenger ﷺ as saying, "If any of you leaves his bed and then comes back to it he should dust his bedding with the inner extremity of his garment three times, for he does not know what has come on to it since he left it. On laying down he should say:

بِاسْمِكَ رَبِّي وَضَعْتُ جَنْبِي وَبِكَ أَرْفَعُهُ ، فَإِنْ أَمْسَكْتَ
نَفْسِي فَارْحَمْهَا ، وَإِنْ أَرْسَلْتَهَا فَاحْفَظْهَا بِمَا تَحْفَظُ بِهِ
عِبَادَكَ الصَّالِحِينَ

'In Your name, my Lord, I lay down my side and by You I raise it up. If You keep my soul, then have mercy on it, but if You let it go, guard it with that which You guard Your right-acting slaves.'"

A version says, "When one of you wakes up let him say:

الْحَمْدُ لِلَّهِ الَّذِي عَافَانِي فِي جَسَدِي وَرَدَّ عَلَيَّ رُوحِي ،
وَأَذِنَ لِي بِذِكْرِهِ

'Praise be to Allah who gave me well-being in my body and returned my spirit to me and allowed me to remember Him.'" (Bukhari, Muslim)

35. ᶜAli ﷺ said that Fatimah ﷺ went to the Prophet ﷺ to request from him a servant, but did not find him. So, finding

ᶜA'ishah, she mentioned the matter to her. ᶜAli said, "The Prophet ﷺ came to us when we had gone to bed and said, 'Shall I not point out to you something better than having a servant? When you go to bed, say, سُبْحَانَ اللَّهِ "Glory be to Allah" thirty-three times, الْحَمْدُ لِلَّهِ "Praise be to Allah" thirty-three times, and اللَّهُ أَكْبَرُ "Allah is most great" thirty-four times. That will be better for you than a servant.'" ᶜAli said, "I have not failed to say them since I heard it from the Messenger of Allah ﷺ." He was asked, "Not even on the night of [the battle of] Siffin?" He said, "Not even on the night of Siffin." (Bukhari, Muslim)

"It has reached us that whoever says these words regularly, weakness will not overcome him in anything that concerns him such as work and the like."

36. Hafsah Umm al-Mu'minin ﷺ said that when Allah's Messenger ﷺ wanted to go to sleep he would put his right hand under his cheek, and then say:

$$ اَللَّهُمَّ قِنِي عَذَابَكَ يَوْمَ تَبْعَثُ عِبَادَكَ $$

"O Allah, guard me from Your punishment on the day when You raise up Your slaves," three times. (Abu Dawud. At-Tirmidhi said, "It is a hasan sahih hadith," and he transmitted it from Hudhaifah ﷺ.)

37. Anas ﷺ said that when the Prophet ﷺ went to his bed he would say:

$$ الْحَمْدُ لِلَّهِ الَّذِي أَطْعَمَنَا وَسَقَانَا وَكَفَانَا وَآوَانَا ، فَكَمْ مِمَّنْ لَا كَافِيَ لَهُ وَلَا مُؤْوِيَ $$

"Praise be to Allah who has fed us, given us drink, satisfied us and given us shelter. Many are those who have no one to provide sufficiency for them, or give them shelter." (Muslim)

38. It is related from Ibn ʿUmar ؓ that he told a man that when he went to bed, he should say:

اَللَّهُمَّ أَنْتَ خَلَقْتَ نَفْسِي ، وَأَنْتَ تَتَوَفَّاهَا ، لَكَ مَمَاتُهَا وَمَحْيَاهَا ، إِنْ أَحْيَيْتَهَا فَاحْفَظْهَا ، وَإِنْ أَمَتَّهَا فَاغْفِرْ لَهَا ، اَللَّهُمَّ أَسْأَلُكَ الْعَافِيَةَ

"O Allah, You created my soul and You will take it, to You belongs its death and its life; if You keep it alive, protect it, but if You give it death, forgive it. O Allah, I ask You for well-being."

Ibn ʿUmar said, "I heard this from the Messenger of Allah ﷺ."
(Muslim)

39. Abu Saʿid al-Khudri said: Allah's Messenger ﷺ said, "Whoever says when going to bed:

أَسْتَغْفِرُ اللَّهَ الْعَظِيمَ الَّذِي لاَ إِلَهَ إِلاَّ هُوَ الْحَيُّ الْقَيُّومُ وَأَتُوبُ إِلَيْهِ

'I ask forgiveness of Allah besides whom there is no god, the Living, the Eternal, and I turn in repentance to Him,'

three times, Allah will forgive him his wrong actions, even if they are like the foam of the sea, or in number like the sand of ʿAlij (a place known for its accumulated sand), and even if they are as numerous as the days of this world." (At-Tirmidhi transmitted it and said, "This is a *hasan gharib hadith*.")

40. Abu Hurairah ؓ said that when the Prophet ﷺ went to his bed he used to say:

اَللَّهُمَّ رَبَّ السَّمَوَاتِ ، وَرَبَّ الأَرْضِ ، وَرَبَّ الْعَرْشِ الْعَظِيمِ ، رَبَّنَا وَرَبَّ كُلِّ شَيْءٍ ، فَالِقَ الْحَبِّ وَالنَّوَى ، وَمُنَزِّلَ التَّوْرَاةِ وَالإِنْجِيلِ وَالْفُرْقَانِ ، أَعُوذُ بِكَ مِنْ شَرِّ

كُلِّ ذِي شَرٍّ أَنْتَ آخِذٌ بِنَاصِيَتِهِ ، اَللَّهُمَّ أَنْتَ الْأَوَّلُ فَلَيْسَ
قَـبْلَكَ شَيْءٌ ، وَأَنْتَ الْآخِـرُ فَلَيْسَ بَعْـدَكَ شَيْءٌ ، وَأَنْتَ
الظَّاهِرُ فَلَيْسَ فَوْقَكَ شَيْءٌ ، وَأَنْتَ الْبَـاطِنُ فَلَيْسَ دُونَكَ
شَيْءٌ ، اقْضِ عَنَّا الدَّيْنَ ، وَأَغْنِنَا مِنَ الْفَقْرِ

"O Allah, Lord of the heavens, Lord of the earth, Lord of the Great Throne, our Lord and Lord of every thing, who split the grain and the date-stone, who sent down the Torah, the Injil and the Qur'an, I seek refuge in You from the mischief of every evil agent whose forelock You seize. You are the First and there is nothing before You; You are the Last and there is nothing after You; You are the Outwardly Apparent and there is nothing over You; You are the Inward and there is nothing beyond You. Pay the debt for us and make us free of need." (Muslim)

41. Al-Bara' ibn ʿAzib ﷺ said: Allah's Messenger ﷺ said to me, "Perform the ablution for prayer when you go to bed, then lie down on your right side, and say:

اَللَّهُمَّ أَسْلَمْتُ نَفْسِي إِلَيْكَ ، وَوَجَّـهْتُ وَجْـهِي إِلَيْكَ ،
وَفَوَّضْتُ أَمْرِي إِلَيْكَ ، وَأَلْجَأْتُ ظَهْرِي إِلَيْكَ رَغْبَةً وَرَهْبَةً
إِلَيْكَ ، لاَ مَلْجَأَ وَلاَ مَنْجَا مِنْكَ إِلاَّ إِلَيْكَ ، آمَنْتُ بِكِتَابِكَ
الَّذِي أَنْزَلْتَ ، وَبِنَبِيِّكَ الَّذِي أَرْسَلْتَ

'O Allah, I have handed over my self to You, turned my face to You, entrusted my affairs to You, and fall back on You out of desire for You and fear of You. There is no refuge and no place of safety from You except by turning to You. I believe in Your Book which You have sent down and in Your Prophet whom You have sent.'"

He added, "If you die during the night you will die in the (*fitrah*) natural state (or the true religion), so make these words the last of what you say [before you sleep]." (Bukhari, Muslim)

5. What one says when he wakes up from sleep at night

42. ᶜUbadah ibn as-Samit ﷺ reported the Prophet ﷺ as saying, "If anyone is disturbed [from sleep] during the night and says:

لاَ إِلَهَ إِلاَّ اللَّهُ وَحْدَهُ لاَ شَرِيكَ لَهُ ، لَهُ الْمُلْكُ ، وَلَهُ الْحَمْدُ ، وَهُوَ عَلَى كُلِّ شَيْءٍ قَدِيرٌ ، وَسُبْحَانُ اللَّهِ ، وَلاَ إِلَهَ إِلاَّ اللَّهُ ، وَاللَّهُ أَكْبَرُ ، وَلاَ حَوْلَ وَلاَ قُوَّةَ إِلاَّ بِاللَّهِ الْعَلِيِّ الْعَظِيمِ

'There is no god but Allah alone without partner; to Him belongs the dominion, to Him praise is due, and He is omnipotent; glory be to Allah; praise be to Allah; there is no god but Allah; Allah is most great; there is no might and no power but in Allah, the Exalted the Vast,' then says:

اَللَّهُمَّ اغْفِرْ لِي

'O Allah, forgive me,'

(or he said, 'Then makes supplication'), his plea will be answered; and if he performs ablution and offers prayer, his prayer will be accepted." (Bukhari)

43. Abu Umamah ﷺ said: I heard Allah's Messenger ﷺ say, "If anyone goes to bed in a state of purity and makes mention of Allah till drowsiness overtakes him, he will not turn round at any time during the night and ask Allah at that time for some of the good of this world and the next without His giving it to him." (At-Tirmidhi transmitted it saying, "This is a *hasan gharib hadith*.")

44. ᶜA'ishah ﷺ said that Allah's Messenger ﷺ when he awoke during the night used to say:

لاَ إِلَهَ إِلاَّ أَنْتَ سُبْحَانَكَ اللَّهُمَّ ، أَسْتَغْفِرُكَ لِذَنْبِي ،

وَأَسْأَلُكَ رَحْمَتَكَ ، اَللَّهُمَّ زِدْنِي عِلْمًا ، وَلاَ تُزِغْ قَلْبِي بَعْدَ إِذْ هَدَيْتَنِي ، وَهَبْ لِي مِنْ لَدُنْكَ رَحْمَةً إِنَّكَ أَنْتَ الْوَهَّابُ

"There is no god but You. Glory be to You, O Allah, I ask for Your forgiveness of my wrong action, and I ask for Your mercy. O Allah, increase me in knowledge, and do not cause my heart to swerve after You have guided me. Grant me mercy from Yourself, You are indeed the Ever-giving One." (Abu Dawud)

45. Abu Hurairah ؓ reported that the Prophet ﷺ said, "When one of you wakes up, let him say:

الْحَمْدُ لِلَّهِ الَّذِي رَدَّ عَلَيَّ رُوحِي ، وَعَافَانِي فِي جَسَدِي

'Praise be to Allah, who returned my spirit to me and gave me well-being in my body.'"

(See *hadith* 34 which has almost exactly the same wording but in a different order.)

46. Anas ؓ said: We were commanded to do *istighfar* (ask forgiveness) at night seventy times.

6. What one who is disturbed and frightened in sleep says

47. Buraidah ؓ said: Khalid ibn al-Walid complained to the Prophet ﷺ "Messenger of Allah, I don't sleep at night because of insomnia." The Prophet ﷺ said to him, "When you go to bed say:

اَللَّهُمَّ رَبَّ السَّمَوَاتِ السَّبْعِ وَمَا أَظَلَّتْ ، وَرَبَّ الأَرْضِينَ السَّبْعِ وَمَا أَقَلَّتْ ، وَرَبَّ الشَّيَاطِينِ وَمَا أَضَلَّتْ ، كُنْ لِي جَارًا مِنْ شَرِّ خَلْقِكَ كُلِّهِمْ جَمِيعًا ، أَنْ يَفْرُطَ أَحَدٌ مِنْهُمْ عَلَيَّ ، وَأَنْ يَبْغِيَ عَلَيَّ ، عَزَّ جَارُكَ ، وَجَلَّ ثَنَاؤُكَ ، وَلاَ إِلَهَ غَيْرُكَ ، وَلاَ إِلَهَ إِلاَّ أَنْتَ

'O Allah, Lord of the seven heavens and what they overshadow, Lord of the lands and what they carry, Lord of the Shaytans and what they lead astray, be a Protector to me from the mischief of all Your creatures lest any of them do mischief or act wrongfully to me. Strong is Your protection and glorious is Your praise. There is no god other than You. There is no god but You.'"
(At-Tirmidhi)

48. ʿAmr ibn Shuʿaib, on his father's authority, said that his grandfather reported that Allah's Messenger ﷺ used to teach them to say whenever frightened in sleep:

أَعُوذُ بِكَلِمَاتِ اللَّهِ التَّامَّةِ مِنْ غَضَبِهِ وَشَرِّ عِبَادِهِ ، وَمِنْ هَمَزَاتِ الشَّيَاطِينِ وَأَنْ يَحْضُرُونِ

"I seek refuge in Allah's perfect words from His anger, the mischief of His slaves, the evil suggestions of the Shaytans and [I seek refuge with You lest] they should attend me."

ʿAbdullah ibn ʿAmr used to teach this *duʿa* to those of his children who were able to learn it. For those [minors] who could not learn it, he [wrote it down and] hung it on the child's neck. (Abu Dawud and at-Tirmidhi transmitted it. At-Tirmidhi said, "This is a *hasan hadith*.")

7. On having a dream

49. Abu Salamah ibn ʿAbd ar-Rahman narrated: I heard Abu Qatadah ibn ar-Rabʿi saying, "I heard the Messenger of Allah ﷺ say, 'Vision is from Allah, and the [bad] dream is from Shaytan. If one of you sees something he dislikes, let him spit three times on his left side, and let him seek refuge in Allah from its mischief, for it will not harm him, Allah willing.'"

Abu Salamah said, "I used to see visions that were heavier on me than a mountain but when I heard this *hadith* I did not worry any more."

In another version he said, "I used to see visions that would worry me until I heard Abu Qatadah saying, 'I used to see visions which would make me ill, until I heard the Messenger of Allah ﷺ say, "The good vision is from Allah. If one of you sees that which he likes, let him not tell it except to whomever he loves. If he sees what he dislikes, let him not tell it to anyone, but let him spit on his left three times and seek refuge with Allah from the accursed Shaytan, from the mischief of what he saw, for it will not harm him.""" (Bukhari, Muslim)

50. Jabir ؓ reported Allah's Messenger ﷺ as saying, "When one of you sees a vision which he dislikes, he must spit on his left three times, seek refuge in Allah from the Shaytan three times, and turn over from the side on which he was lying." (Muslim)

51. It is mentioned that a man related his vision to the Prophet ﷺ and the Prophet ﷺ said, "Good you have seen and good it will be."[1] In another version he said, "Good you will meet, and mischief you will be protected from; it is good for us and evil for our enemies, and all praise belongs to Allah, the Lord of all the worlds."[2]

8. On the excellence of *ibadah* (worship) at night

Allah, exalted is He, says:

$$ يَا أَيُّهَا الْمُزَّمِّلُ قُمِ اللَّيْلَ إِلاَّ قَلِيلاً $$

up until His words:

$$ إِنَّ نَاشِئَةَ اللَّيْلِ هِيَ أَشَدُّ وَطْأً وَأَقْوَمُ قِيلاً $$

"O you wrapped up in your cloak, stand [in prayer] at night except for a little...the vigil of the night is [a time] when impression is more keen and speech more certain."
(Qur'an, al-Muzzammil: 1-5)

---

[1] It is weak; Ibn as-Sunni transmitted it.

[2] It is very weak; Ibn as-Sunni transmitted it.

And He says, exalted is He:

وَمِنَ اللَّيْلِ فَتَهَجَّدْ بِهِ نَافِلَةً لَكَ عَسَى أَنْ يَبْعَثَكَ رَبُّكَ مَقَامًا مَحْمُودًا

"And some part of the night awake for it, as an optional act for you, perhaps your Lord will raise you to a praised station."
(Qur'an, al-Isra': 79)

And He says, exalted is He:

وَمِنَ اللَّيْلِ فَاسْجُدْ لَهُ وَسَبِّحْهُ لَيْلاً طَويلاً

"And prostrate to Him [a portion] of the night. And glorify Him through the livelong night."
(Qur'an, ad-Dahr: 26)

52. Abu Hurairah ﷺ reported that the Prophet ﷺ said, "Our Lord descends every night to the lowest heaven when the last third of the night remains and says, 'Who calls Me so that I may answer him? Who asks Me so that I may give him? Who asks My forgiveness so that I may forgive him?'" (Bukhari, Muslim)

53. ʿAmr ibn ʿAbsah ﷺ reported that he heard the Prophet ﷺ saying, "The Lord is nearest to the slave in the course of the last part of the night, so if you are able to be among those who remember Allah at that hour, do so." (At-Tirmidhi transmitted it, saying, "This is a *hasan hadith* and it is *sahih*.")

54. Jabir ﷺ said: I heard the Prophet ﷺ say, "During the night there is an hour in which no Muslim man will ask Allah, Mighty and Majestic is He, for good in this world and the next without His giving it to him; and that is every night." (Muslim)

And Allah, exalted is He, says:

وَالْمُسْتَغْفِرِينَ بِالْأَسْحَارِ

"And those who pray for pardon in the watches of the night."

(Qur'an, Al ʿImran: 17)

55. It is mentioned of Anas ibn Malik ﷺ that he said: We were commanded to ask forgiveness (do *istighfar*) at night seventy times.

9. A supplement on what one says when one wakes up

56. Abu Hurairah ﷺ reported that the Prophet ﷺ said, "When one of you wakes up he should say:

الْحَمْدُ لِلَّهِ الَّذِي رَدَّ عَلَيَّ رُوحِي ، وَعَافَانِي فِي جَسَدِي ،
وَأَذِنَ لِي بِذِكْرِهِ

'Praise be to Allah who returned my soul to me and gave me vigour in my body and allowed me to remember Him.'" [1]

57. He [Abu Hurairah] ﷺ also said: Allah's Messenger ﷺ said, "No man wakes up and says:

الْحَمْدُ لِلَّهِ الَّذِي خَلَقَ النَّوْمَ وَالْيَقَظَةَ ، الْحَمْدُ لِلَّهِ الَّذِي
بَعَثَنِي سَالِمًا سَوِيًّا ، أَشْهَدُ أَنَّ اللَّهَ يُحْيِي الْمَوْتَى وَهُوَ
عَلَى كُلِّ شَيْءٍ قَدِيرٌ

'Praise belongs to Allah who created sleep and wakefulness, praise belongs to Allah who raised me up safe and sound. I witness that Allah brings the dead to life and He has Power over everything,'

---

[1] See *ahadith* nos. 34 and 45.

but that Allah says, 'My slave has told the truth.'"[1]

58. Anas ﷺ said: Allah's Messenger ﷺ said, "Whoever says –
meaning when he leaves his house:

$$\text{بِسْمِ اللَّهِ ، تَوَكَّلْتُ عَلَى اللَّهِ ، لاَ حَوْلَ وَلاَ قُوَّةَ إِلاَّ بِاللَّهِ}$$

> 'In the name of Allah; I place my trust in Allah; there is no
> might and no power except by Allah,"

the following will be said to him [at that time], 'You will be sufficed,
protected and guided.' The Shaytan will go far from him and will
say to another Shaytan, 'How can you deal with a man who has
been guided, sufficed, and protected?'" (Abu Dawud, an-Nasa'i
and at-Tirmidhi transmitted it. At-Tirmidhi said, "This is a *hasan
sahih hadith*.")

59. Umm Salamah ﷺ said: Allah's Messenger ﷺ never went
out of my house without raising his eyes to the sky and saying:

$$\text{اَللَّهُمَّ أَعُوذُ بِكَ أَنْ أَضِلَّ أَوْ أُضَلَّ ، أَوْ أَزِلَّ أَوْ أُزَلَّ ، أَوْ أَظْلِمَ}$$
$$\text{أَوْ أُظْلَمَ ، أَوْ أَجْهَلَ أَوْ يُجْهَلَ عَلَيَّ}$$

> "O Allah, I seek refuge with You lest I stray or be led astray, or
> I slip or be caused to slip, or cause injustice, or suffer injustice,
> or behave foolishly or have others behave foolishly to me."

(Abu Dawud, an-Nasa'i, Ibn Majah and at-Tirmidhi transmitted
it. At-Tirmidhi said, "This is a *hasan sahih hadith*.")

10. On entering the house

60. Jabir ibn ʿAbdullah said: I heard the Prophet ﷺ saying, "When
a man enters his house and mentions Allah's name on entering and
when eating his food, the Shaytan says [to his companions], "You
have no place to spend the night and no evening meal"; but when

---

[1] A very weak *hadith*; Ibn as-Sunni transmitted it.

he enters without remembering Allah, exalted is He, on entering the house, the Shaytan says [to his companions], "You have found a place to spend the night"; and when he does not remember Allah, exalted is He, upon eating his food, he says, "You have found a place to spend the night and an evening meal." (Muslim)

61. Abu Malik al-Ash'ari ؓ said: Allah's Messenger ﷺ said, "When a man enters his house he should say:

اَللَّهُمَّ إِنِّي أَسْأَلُكَ خَيْرَ الْمَوْلَجِ ، وَخَيْرَ الْمَخْرَجِ ، بِسْمِ اللَّهِ خَرَجْنَا ، وَعَلَى اللَّهِ رَبِّنَا تَوَكَّلْنَا

'O Allah, I ask You for good both when entering and when going out; in the name of Allah we enter, in the name of Allah we come out, and in Allah our Lord do we put our trust.'
He should then greet his family." (Abu Dawud)

62. Anas ؓ said: Allah's Messenger ﷺ said to me, "My little son! Give a greeting when you go in to your family. It will be a blessing both to you and to the members of your family." (At-Tirmidhi transmitted it, saying, "This is a *hasan sahih hadith*.")

11. On entering the mosque and coming out of it

63. It is related from Anas ؓ and others that when the Messenger of Allah ﷺ entered the mosque he would say:

بِسْمِ اللَّهِ ، اَللَّهُمَّ صَلِّ عَلَى مُحَمَّدٍ

"In the name of Allah, O Allah bless Muhammad,"
and when he came out he would say:

"In the name of Allah, O Allah bless Muhammad."[1]

---

[1] A *hasan hadith*; Ibn as-Sunni transmitted it.

64. Abu Humaid or Abu Usaid ﵁ said: Allah's Messenger ﷺ said, "When any of you enters the mosque he should invoke blessings on the Prophet and say:

اَللَّهُمَّ افْتَحْ لِي أَبْوَابَ رَحْمَتِكَ

'O Allah, open to me the doors of Your mercy,'
and when he goes out he should say:

اَللَّهُمَّ إِنِّي أَسْأَلُكَ مِنْ فَضْلِكَ

'O Allah, I ask You of Your bounty.'" (A *sahih hadith*. Muslim transmitted it in similar words.)

65. ʿAbdullah ibn ʿAmr ﵁, said that Allah's Messenger ﷺ used to say on entering the mosque:

أَعُوذُ بِاللَّهِ الْعَظِيمِ ، وَبِوَجْهِهِ الْكَرِيمِ ، وَبِسُلْطَانِهِ الْقَدِيمِ
مِنَ الشَّيْطَانِ الرَّجِيمِ

"I seek refuge with Allah the Tremendous, with His noble Face and His eternal power from the accursed Shaytan."
He said, "When one says this, the Shaytan says, 'He is protected from me for the rest of the day.'" (Abu Dawud)

12. On the *adhan* and hearing it

66. Abu Hurairah ﵁ said: Allah's Messenger ﷺ said, "If people knew what [blessing] lies in the call to prayer and in the first row [of prayer], and they could do nothing but cast lots for it, they would cast lots for it." (Bukhari, Muslim)

67. Abu Hurairah ﵁ reported Allah's Messenger ﷺ as saying, "When a summons to prayer is made the Shaytan turns his back and breaks wind so as not to hear the *adhan*. When the *adhan* is finished he turns round. When a second call to prayer (*iqamah*) is

made he turns his back, and when the second call is finished he turns round to distract a man, saying, 'Remember such and such; remember such and such,' referring to something he had forgotten, with the result that he does not know how much he has prayed." (Bukhari, Muslim)

68. Abu Saᶜid ﷺ said: I heard Allah's Messenger ﷺ saying, "All jinn, men, or any other thing, who hear the voice of the *mu'adhdhin* as far away as it is possible to hear it, will testify on his behalf on the day of resurrection." (Bukhari)

69. Abu Saᶜid ﷺ reported the Messenger of Allah ﷺ as saying, "When you hear the *adhan* repeat what the *mu'adhdhin* says." (Bukhari, Muslim)

70. ᶜAbdullah ibn ᶜAmr ﷺ reported that he heard Allah's Messenger ﷺ saying, "When you hear the *mu'adhdhin* repeat what he says, then invoke blessing on me, for, everyone who invokes a blessing on me, Allah will send ten blessings on him for it. Then ask Allah to give me the *wasilah*, which is a degree in the Garden which will only be granted to one of Allah's slaves, and I hope that I may be him. If anyone asks that I be given the *wasilah* he will be assured of [my] intercession." (Muslim)

71. ᶜUmar ibn al-Khattab ﷺ said: Allah's Messenger ﷺ said, "When the *mu'adhdhin* says, اَللَّهُ أَكْبَرُ ، اَللَّهُ أَكْبَرُ 'Allah is most great, Allah is most great,' and one of you responds:

$$اَللَّهُ أَكْبَرُ ، اَللَّهُ أَكْبَرُ$$

'Allah is most great, Allah is most great';
then he says, أَشْهَدُ أَنْ لَا إِلَهَ إِلَّا اللَّهُ 'I witness that there is no god but Allah,' and he responds:

$$أَشْهَدُ أَنْ لَا إِلَهَ إِلَّا اللَّهُ$$

'I testify that there is no god but Allah';

then he says, أَشْهَدُ أَنَّ مُحَمَّدًا رَسُولُ اللَّهِ 'I witness that Muhammad is Allah's Messenger,' and he responds:

$$ أَشْهَدُ أَنَّ مُحَمَّدًا رَسُولُ اللَّهِ $$

'I witness that Muhammad is Allah's Messenger';

then he says, حَيَّ عَلَى الصَّلَاةِ 'Come to prayer,' and he responds:

$$ لَا حَوْلَ وَلَا قُوَّةَ إِلَّا بِاللَّهِ $$

'There is no might and no strength except by Allah';

then he says, حَيَّ عَلَى الْفَلَاحِ 'Come to success,' and he responds:

$$ لَا حَوْلَ وَلَا قُوَّةَ إِلَّا بِاللَّهِ $$

'There is no might and no strength except by Allah';

then he says, اللَّهُ أَكْبَرُ ، اللَّهُ أَكْبَرُ 'Allah is most great, Allah is most great' and he responds:

$$ اللَّهُ أَكْبَرُ ، اللَّهُ أَكْبَرُ $$

'Allah is most great, Allah is most great'; v. v-good

then he says, لَا إِلَهَ إِلَّا اللَّهُ 'There is no god but Allah', and he makes the response:

$$ لَا إِلَهَ إِلَّا اللَّهُ $$

'There is no god but Allah';

[saying this] from his heart, he will enter the Garden." (Muslim)

72. Jabir ﷠ reported Allah's Messenger ﷺ as saying, "If anyone says when he hears the call (*adhan*):

$$ اَللَّهُمَّ رَبَّ هَذِهِ الدَّعْوَةِ التَّامَّةِ ، وَالصَّلَاةِ الْقَائِمَةِ ، آتِ مُحَمَّدًا الْوَسِيلَةَ وَالْفَضِيلَةَ ، وَابْعَثْهُ مَقَامًا مَحْمُودًا الَّذِي وَعَدْتَهُ $$

✳ *'O Allah, Lord of this perfect call and of the prayer which is established [for all time], grant Muhammad the wasilah and excellence and raise him up in a praiseworthy station, the one which You have promised him,'*

he will be assured of my intercession on the day of Resurrection." (Bukhari)

73. ᶜAbdullah ibn ᶜAmr ﷺ told of a man who said, "Messenger of Allah, the *mu'adhdhins* excel us." The Messenger of Allah ﷺ replied, "Say the same words as they say, and when you finish, ask and you will be given." (Abu Dawud)

74. Anas ﷺ reported: Allah's Messenger ﷺ said, "The supplication made between the *adhan* and the *iqamah* is not rejected." They said, "So what should we say, Messenger of Allah?" He said, "Ask Allah for well-being in this world and in the world to come." (At-Tirmidhi transmitted it, saying, "This is a *hasan sahih hadith*.")

75. Sahl ibn Saᶜd ﷺ said: Allah's Messenger ﷺ said, "Two things are not rejected, or are seldom rejected: a supplication when the call to prayer is made, and in the heat of the battle when people are slaughtering each other." (Abu Dawud)

76. Umm Salamah ﷺ said: Allah's Messenger ﷺ taught me to say, when the *adhan* for the sunset prayer was called:

اَللّٰهُمَّ هٰذَا إِقْبَالُ لَيْلِكَ ، وَإِدْبَارُ نَهَارِكَ ، وَأَصْوَاتُ دُعَاتِكَ ، وَحُضُورُ صَلَوَاتِكَ ، فَاغْفِرْ لِي

✳ *"O Allah, this is the advent of Your night, and the retreat of Your day, [and these are] the voices of Your summoners, and those who attend Your prayers, so forgive me." (Abu Dawud, at-Tirmidhi)*

77. One of the Companions of Allah's Messenger ﷺ said that Bilal began the *iqamah*. When he said:

$$\text{قَدْ قَامَتِ الصَّلَاةُ}$$

✳ *"The prayer is established,"*
Allah's Messenger ﷺ said:

$$\text{أَقَامَهَا اللَّهُ وَأَدَامَهَا}$$

✳✳ *"May Allah establish it and cause it to continue."* (Abu Dawud)

13. On beginning the prayer

78. Abu Hurairah ؓ said: Allah's Messenger ﷺ when he began the prayer used to keep silent for a little while before reciting [the Qur'an]. So I said, "Messenger of Allah, may my parents be sacrificed for you! In the pause between the *takbir* and recitation what do you say?" He said, "I say:

$$\text{اَللَّهُمَّ بَاعِدْ بَيْنِي وَبَيْنَ خَطَايَايَ كَمَا بَاعَدْتَ بَيْنَ الْمَشْرِقِ}$$
$$\text{وَالْمَغْرِبِ ، اَللَّهُمَّ نَقِّنِي مِنْ خَطَايَايَ كَمَا يُنَقَّى الثَّوْبُ}$$
$$\text{الْأَبْيَضُ مِنَ الدَّنَسِ ، اَللَّهُمَّ اغْسِلْنِي مِنْ خَطَايَايَ بِالثَّلْجِ}$$
$$\text{وَالْمَاءِ وَالْبَرَدِ}$$

'O Allah! Put a distance between me and my wrong actions as You have placed a distance between the East and West, and cleanse me of my wrong actions as a white garment is cleansed of dirt [after thorough washing]. O Allah! Wash off my wrong actions with water, snow and hail.'" (Bukhari, Muslim)

79. Jubair ibn Mut'im ؓ said that he saw Allah's Messenger ﷺ performing a prayer [in which] he said:

$$\text{اللَّهُ أَكْبَرُ كَبِيرًا ، وَالْحَمْدُ لِلَّهِ كَثِيرًا ، وَسُبْحَانَ اللَّهِ بُكْرَةً}$$

وَأَصِيـلاً (ثَلاَثًا)، أَعُـوذُ بِـاللهِ مِنَ الشَّيْطَانِ الرَّجِيمِ ، مِنْ
نَفْخِهِ وَنَفْثِهِ وَهَمْزِهِ

*"Allah is altogether great; praise be to Allah in abundance;
glory be to Allah in the morning and afternoon (saying it three
times). I seek refuge with Allah from the accursed Shaytan,
from his puffing up (nafkh), his spitting (nafth), and his evil
suggestion (hamz)." His puffing up is pride, his spitting is
poetry and his evil suggestion is death.* (Abu Dawud)

80. ʿA'ishah ﷽ and Abu Saʿid and others ﷽, related that
when Allah's Messenger ﷺ began to pray he said:

سُبْحَانَكَ اللَّهُمَّ وَبِحَمْدِكَ ، وَتَبَارَكَ اسْمُكَ ، وَتَعَالَى جَدُّكَ
، وَلاَ إِلَهَ غَيْرُكَ

*"Glory be to You, O Allah, and with praise to You [do I begin
my worship]. Blessed is Your name, exalted is Your majesty,
and there is no god other than You."* (At-Tirmidhi, Abu Dawud,
Ibn Majah and an-Nasa'i transmitted it)

81. It is related from ʿUmar ﷽ that he said, *"Allahu Akbar"*
(Allah is most great) and he started his prayer with it (the above
duʿa). (Muslim)

82. ʿAli ﷽ said that when Allah's Messenger ﷺ stood up for
prayer, he said:

وَجَّهْتُ وَجْهِيَ لِلَّذِي فَطَرَ السَّمَـوَاتِ وَالأَرْضَ حَنِيفًا وَمَا
أَنَا مِنَ الْمُشْرِكِينَ ، إِنَّ صَلاتِي وَنُسُكِي وَمَحْيَايَ وَمَمَاتِي
لِلّٰهِ رَبِّ الْعَـالَمِينَ ، لاَ شَـرِيكَ لَهُ وَبِذَلِكَ أُمِرْتُ وَأَنَا مِنَ
الْمُسْلِمِينَ ، اَللَّهُمَّ أَنْتَ الْمَلِكُ ، لاَ إِلَهَ إِلاَّ أَنْتَ ، أَنْتَ رَبِّي
وَأَنَا عَبْدُكَ ، ظَلَمْتُ نَفْسِي ، وَاعْتَرَفْتُ بِذَنْبِي ، فَاغْفِرْلِي

41

ذُنُوبِي جَمِيعًا ، إِنَّهُ لَا يَغْفِرُ الذُّنُوبَ إِلَّا أَنْتَ ، وَاهْدِنِي
لِأَحْسَنِ الْأَخْلَاقِ ، لَا يَهْدِي لِأَحْسَنِهَا إِلَّا أَنْتَ ، وَاصْرِفْ عَنِّي
سَيِّئَهَا لَا يَصْرِفُ عَنِّي سَيِّئَهَا إِلَّا أَنْتَ ، لَبَّيْكَ وَسَعْدَيْكَ ،
وَالْخَيْرُ كُلُّهُ فِي يَدَيْكَ ، وَالشَّرُّ لَيْسَ إِلَيْكَ ، أَنَا بِكَ
وَإِلَيْكَ ، تَبَارَكْتَ وَتَعَالَيْتَ ، أَسْتَغْفِرُكَ وَأَتُوبُ إِلَيْكَ

"I have turned my face as a hanif (one by nature inclined to the Truth) towards Him who created the heavens and the earth, and I am not one who associates partners with Allah. My prayer and my devotion, my life and my death belong to Allah the Lord of the Universe, who has no partner. That is what I have been commanded, and I am one of the Muslims. O Allah, You are the King. There is no god but You. You are my Lord and I am Your slave. I have wronged myself, and I acknowledge my wrong action, so forgive me all my wrong actions, for none forgives wrong actions but You; and guide me to the best qualities of character, for none guides to the best of them but You; and avert the bad qualities [of character] from me, for none averts the bad of them from me but You. I come to serve and please You. All good is in Your hands and evil does not pertain to You. I [exist] by You and [am returning] to You, blessed are You and greatly exalted, I seek Your forgiveness and I turn in repentance to You."

Know that the school of the people of truth among the scholars of hadith, and the people of fiqh among the Companions and the Followers and those who came after them of the people of knowledge among the Muslims is that all beings, the good of them and the bad of them, their benefit and their harm, all of them are from Allah, exalted is He, and they are by His will and His decree. So we must interpret this hadith (i.e. "and evil does not pertain to You"). The people of knowledge have mentioned some answers to it:

First of which and the most famous is that which an-Nadr ibn

Shumail and other Imams after him said, that its meaning is, "Nearness cannot be sought to You [through it]."

Second, "It [evil] does not ascend to You, but it is only al-Kalim at-Tayyib (the Good Words) which ascend."

Third, "It must not be attributed to You, out of courtesy. One cannot say, 'O Creator of Evil!' even though He is the Creator of it, just as one cannot say, 'O Creator of pigs!' even though He is their Creator."

Fourth, "It [evil] is not evil from the point of view of Your wisdom, for You do not create anything without purpose.")

(Muslim transmitted it, commenting. "It is said that it was in the night prayer.")

83. Something that has also been narrated about the night prayer (the *tahajjud*) is the *hadith* of ʿAʾishah that she said: When Allah's Messenger got up at night he began his prayer by saying:

اَللَّهُمَّ رَبَّ جِبْرِيلَ ، وَمِيكَائِيلَ ، وَإِسْرَافِيلَ ، فَاطِرَ السَّمَوَاتِ وَالأَرْضِ ، عَالِمَ الْغَيْبِ وَالشَّهَادَةِ ، أَنْتَ تَحْكُمُ بَيْنَ عِبَادِكَ فِيمَا كَانُوا يَخْتَلِفُونَ ، اهْدِنِي لِمَا اخْتُلِفَ فِيهِ مِنَ الْحَقِّ بِإِذْنِكَ ، إِنَّكَ تَهْدِي مَنْ تَشَاءُ إِلَى صِرَاطٍ مُسْتَقِيمٍ

"O Allah, Lord of Jibril, Mika'il and Israfil, Creator of the heavens and the earth, Knower of the unseen and the seen, You judge between Your slaves concerning their differences. Guide me to the truth of that about which there are different opinions, by Your permission; verily You guide whom You will to a straight path." (Muslim)

84. Ibn ʿAbbas said: Allah's Messenger said when he got up during the night to pray:

اَللَّهُمَّ لَكَ الْحَمْدُ ، أَنْتَ نُورُ السَّمَوَاتِ وَالأَرْضِ وَمَنْ فِيهِنَّ ، وَلَكَ الْحَمْدُ ، أَنْتَ قَيَّامُ السَّمَوَاتِ وَالأَرْضِ وَمَنْ فِيهِنَّ ، وَلَكَ الْحَمْدُ ، أَنْتَ رَبُّ السَّمَوَاتِ وَالأَرْضِ وَمَنْ فِيهِنَّ ، [وَلَكَ الْحَمْدُ] أَنْتَ الْحَقُّ ، وَوَعْدُكَ الْحَقُّ ، وَقَوْلُكَ الْحَقُّ ، وَلِقَاَئُكَ حَقٌّ ، وَالْجَنَّةُ حَقٌّ ، وَالنَّارُ حَقٌّ ، وَالنَّبِيُّونَ حَقٌّ ، وَمُحَمَّدٌ حَقٌّ ، وَالسَّاعَةُ حَقٌّ ، اَللَّهُمَّ لَكَ أَسْلَمْتُ ، وَبِكَ آمَنْتُ ، وَعَلَيْكَ تَوَكَّلْتُ ، وَإِلَيْكَ أَنَبْتُ ، وَبِكَ خَاصَمْتُ ، وَإِلَيْكَ حَاكَمْتُ ، فَاغْفِرْلِي مَا قَدَّمْتُ وَمَا أَخَّرْتُ ، وَمَا أَسْرَرْتُ وَمَا أَعْلَنْتُ ، أَنْتَ إِلَهِي ، لاَ إِلَهَ إِلاَّ أَنْتَ

"O Allah, to You belongs the praise; You are the light of the heavens and the earth and their inhabitants. To You belongs the praise; You are the One by whom the heavens and the earth and their inhabitants exist. To You belongs the praise; You are the Lord of the heavens and the earth and their inhabitants. [To You belongs the praise]; You are the Truth, Your promise is the truth, Your word is the truth, the meeting with You is true, the Garden is true, the Fire is true, the Prophets are true, Muhammad is true, the last Hour is true. O Allah, to You I submit, in You I believe, upon You I depend, to You I repent, by Your help I have disputed, and to You I have come for decision, so forgive me my former and my latter [wrong actions], what I have kept secret and what I have made public. You are my God. There is no God but You." (Bukhari, Muslim)

14. On supplication in the *ruku*, on standing from it, in *sajdah* and between the two *sajdahs*

85. Hudhaifah ﷺ said that he heard the Prophet ﷺ say when bowing:

سُبْحَانَ رَبِّيَ الْعَظِيمِ

✳ *"Glory be to my Lord the Tremendous"*; three times,
and when prostrating himself,

$$سُبْحَانَ رَبِّيَ الأَعْلَى$$

✳ *"Glory be to my Lord the Most High"*; three times.
(At-Tirmidhi, Abu Dawud, an-Nasa'i and Ibn Majah)

86. In the *hadith* of ʿAli ﷺ describing the prayer of Allah's
Messenger ﷺ [he said]: When he bowed, he said:

$$اَللّٰهُمَّ لَكَ رَكَعْتُ ، وَبِكَ آمَنْتُ ، وَلَكَ أَسْلَمْتُ ، خَشَعَ لَكَ
سَمْعِي ، وَبَصَرِي ، وَمُخِّي ، وَعَظْمِي ، وَعَصَبِي$$

*"O Allah to You I bow, in You I believe, and to You I submit
myself. My hearing, my sight, my brain, my bone and my sinews
humble themselves before You."*

When he raised his head he said:

$$سَمِعَ اللّٰهُ لِمَنْ حَمِدَهُ ، رَبَّنَا وَلَكَ الْحَمْدُ ، مِلْءَ السَّمٰوَاتِ
وَمِلْءَ الأَرْضِ ، وَمِلْءَ مَا بَيْنَهُمَا ، وَمِلْءَ مَا شِئْتَ مِنْ
شَيْءٍ بَعْدُ$$

✳ *"Allah hears whoever praises Him, O Allah to You belongs the
praise, as much as the fullness of the heavens, and as much as
the fullness of the earth, and as much as the fullness of what is
between them, and as much as the fullness of whatever else You
will after that."*

When he prostrated himself he said:

$$اَللّٰهُمَّ لَكَ سَجَدْتُ ، وَبِكَ آمَنْتُ ، وَلَكَ أَسْلَمْتُ ، سَجَدَ
وَجْهِي لِلَّذِي خَلَقَهُ وَصَوَّرَهُ ، وَشَقَّ سَمْعَهُ وَبَصَرَهُ ، تَبَارَكَ
اللّٰهُ أَحْسَنُ الْخَالِقِينَ$$

"O Allah, to You I prostrate myself, in You I believe, and to

You I submit myself. My face has prostrated itself to the One who created it, fashioned it, brought forth its hearing and sight. Blessed is Allah, the Best of creators." (Muslim)

87. ʿA'ishah ﷺ told how Allah's Messenger ﷺ often said while bowing and prostrating himself:

سُبْحَانَكَ اَللَّهُمَّ رَبَّنَا وَبِحَمْدِكَ ، اَللَّهُمَّ اغْفِرْلِي

"Glory be to You, O Allah, our Lord, and with Your praise. O Allah forgive me," reflecting [the command in] the Qur'an. (Bukhari, Muslim). *She meant His words, exalted is He, [in Surah an-Nasr],* **"So glorify with praise of your Lord and seek His forgiveness. Truly He is ever ready to show mercy."**

88. ʿA'ishah ﷺ said: Allah's Messenger ﷺ used to say in his bowing and prostration:

سُبُّوحٌ قُدُّوسٌ رَبُّ الْمَلَائِكَةِ وَالرُّوحِ

"All-Glorious, All-Holy, Lord of the angels and the Spirit." (Muslim)

89. Ibn ʿAbbas ﷺ said: Allah's Messenger ﷺ said, "I have been prohibited to recite the Qur'an when bowing or prostrating myself; so when bowing magnify the Lord, and when prostrating yourselves be earnest in supplication, for it is fitting that your supplications should be answered." (Muslim)

90. ʿAwf ibn Malik ﷺ said: One night I stood up to pray along with Allah's Messenger ﷺ. He recited Surah al-Baqarah and when he came across an *ayah* [containing mention] of mercy he stopped and asked [for mercy] and whenever he came to an *ayah* [containing mention] of punishment, he stopped and sought refuge [from it]. He said: Then he bowed about as long as he had stood, saying while bowing:

سُبْحَانَ ذِي الْجَبَرُوتِ وَالْمَلَكُوتِ ، وَالْكِبْرِيَاءِ وَالْعَظَمَةِ

"Glory be to the Possessor of greatness, the kingdom, grandeur
and majesty,"

and he said the same while prostrating. (Abu Dawud, an-Nasa'i)

91. Abu Hurairah said: Allah's Messenger would say:

سَمِعَ اللَّهُ لِمَنْ حَمِدَهُ

"Allah listens to him who praises Him"

when coming to an erect position after bowing, then he would
say while standing:

رَبَّنَا وَلَكَ الْحَمْدُ

"Our Lord, and to You belongs the praise,"

and in another sahih wording:

رَبَّنَا لَكَ الْحَمْدُ

"Our Lord, to You belongs the praise,"

but that which Bukhari and Muslim agree upon is:

رَبَّنَا وَلَكَ الْحَمْدُ

"Our Lord, and to You belongs the praise," and:

اَللَّهُمَّ رَبَّنَا لَكَ الْحَمْدُ

"O Allah, our Lord, to You belongs the praise." (Bukhari,
Muslim)

92. Abu Saʿid al-Khudri said: When Allah's Messenger
raised his head after bowing he said:

اَللَّهُمَّ رَبَّنَا لَكَ الْحَمْدُ ، مِلْءَ السَّمَوَاتِ وَمِلْءَ الأَرْضِ ،
وَمِلْءَ مَا بَيْنَهُمَا ، وَمِلْءَ مَا شِئْتَ مِنْ شَيْءٍ بَعْدُ ، أَهْلَ

الثَّنَاءِ وَالْمَجْدِ ، أَحَقُّ مَا قَالَ الْعَبْدُ ، وَكُلُّنَا لَكَ عَبْدٌ ،
اَللَّهُمَّ لَا مَانِعَ لِمَا أَعْطَيْتَ ، وَلَا مُعْطِيَ لِمَا مَنَعْتَ ، وَلَا
يَنْفَعُ ذَا الْجَدِّ مِنْكَ الْجَدُّ

✴ *"O Allah, our Lord, to You belongs the praise in measure according to the fullness of the heavens and the fullness of the earth and the fullness of what is between them, and the fullness of whatever You will after that. O You who are worthy of praise and glory. This is the truest thing which the slave says – and each of us is Your slave, 'No one can withhold what You give or give what You withhold, and riches cannot avail a wealthy person with You.'"* (Muslim)

93. Rifaᶜah ibn Rafiᶜ said: We were praying behind the Prophet ﷺ and when he raised his head at the end of the *rakᶜah* he said:

سَمِعَ اللَّهُ لِمَنْ حَمِدَهُ

✴ *"Allah listens to him who praises Him."*
A man behind him said:

رَبَّنَا وَلَكَ الْحَمْدُ حَمْدًا كَثِيرًا طَيِّبًا مُبَارَكًا فِيهِ

✴ ✴ *"O our Lord, to You belongs the praise, abundant good praise, blessed in it."*
When he finished he asked, "Who was the speaker just now?" [The man] replied, "I was." He said, "I saw over thirty angels racing one another to be the first to record it." (Bukhari)

94. Abu Hurairah ﷺ reported Allah's Messenger ﷺ as saying, "The nearest a slave comes to his Lord is when he is prostrating himself, so make a great deal of supplication." (Muslim)

95. Abu Hurairah ﷺ said that Allah's Messenger ﷺ used to say when prostrating himself:

اَللّٰهُمَّ اغْـفِـرْلِي ذَنْبِي كُلَّهُ ، دِقَّـهُ وَجِلَّهُ ، وَأَوَّلَهُ وَآخِـرَهُ ، وَعَلاَنِيَهُ وَسِرَّهُ

"O Allah, forgive me all of my wrong action, the small of it and the great of it, the first of it and the last of it, the open of it and the secret of it." (Muslim)

96. ʿA'ishah said: One night I missed Allah's Messenger [from the bed]. So I looked for him and my hand fell on the soles of his feet while he was in the act of prostration with them raised, and he was saying:

اَللّٰهُمَّ إِنِّي أَعُوذُ بِرِضَاكَ مِنْ سَخَطِكَ ، وَبِمُعَافَاتِكَ مِنْ عُـقُوبَتِكَ ، وَأَعُـوذُ بِكَ مِنْكَ ، لاَ أُحْصِي ثَنَاءً عَلَيْكَ ، أَنْتَ كَمَا أَثْنَيْتَ عَلَى نَفْسِكَ

"O Allah, I seek refuge in Your good pleasure from Your anger, and in Your forgiveness from Your punishment, and I seek refuge in You from You. I cannot reckon Your praise, You are as You have praised Yourself." (Muslim)

97. Ibn ʿAbbas said: Allah's Messenger used to say between the two *sajdahs:*

اَللّٰهُمَّ اغْفِرْلِي ، وَارْحَمْنِي ، وَاهْدِنِي ، وَاجْبُرْنِي ، وَعَافِنِي ، وَارْزُقْنِي

"O Allah, forgive me, show mercy to me, guide me, heal me, give me well-being and provide for me." (Abu Dawud and others)

98. In the *hadith* of Hudhaifah there is that Allah's Messenger used to say between the two *sajdahs:*

رَبِّ اغْفِرْلِي ، رَبِّ اغْفِرْلِي

"My Lord, forgive me. My Lord, forgive me." (Abu Dawud and others)

15. On supplication in the prayer and after *tashahhud*

99. Abu Hurairah ﵁ reported Allah's Messenger ﷺ as saying, "When one of you finishes the last *tashahhud* he should seek refuge in Allah from four things: the punishment in Hell, the punishment in the grave, the trials of life and death, and the mischief of the Dajjal Messiah (*Masih* 'Anointed One', *Dajjal* 'Great Liar')." (Muslim)

100. ʿAʾishah ﵂ said that Allah's Messenger ﷺ used to make supplication during the prayer saying:

اَللَّهُمَّ إِنِّي أَعُوذُ بِكَ مِنْ عَذَابِ الْقَبْرِ ، وَأَعُوذُ بِكَ مِنْ فِتْنَةِ الْمَسِيحِ الدَّجَّالِ ، وَأَعُوذُ بِكَ مِنْ فِتْنَةِ الْمَحْيَا وَالْمَمَاتِ ، اَللَّهُمَّ إِنِّي أَعُوذُ بِكَ مِنَ الْمَأْثَمِ وَالْمَغْرَمِ

"O Allah, I seek refuge in You from the punishment in the grave, I seek refuge in You from the trial of the Dajjal Messiah, I seek refuge in You from the trial of life and [the trial] of death. O Allah, I seek refuge in You from wrong action and debt."
Someone said to him, "How often you seek refuge from debt!" He replied, "When a man is in debt, he talks and tells lies, makes promises and breaks them." (Bukhari, Muslim)

101. ʿAbdullah ibn ʿAmr ﵁ reported that Abu Bakr as-Siddiq ﵁ said to Allah's Messenger ﷺ "Teach me a supplication to use in my prayer." He said, "Say:

اَللَّهُمَّ إِنِّي ظَلَمْتُ نَفْسِي ظُلْمًا كَثِيرًا ، وَلاَ يَغْفِرُ الذُّنُوبَ إِلاَّ أَنْتَ ، فَاغْفِرْ لِي مَغْفِرَةً مِنْ عِنْدِكَ ، وَارْحَمْنِي إِنَّكَ أَنْتَ الْغَفُورُ الرَّحِيمُ

'O Allah, I have greatly wronged myself, and You alone can ~~exc))~~
forgive wrong actions, so grant me forgiveness from You and
show mercy to me. You are the Forgiving and the Merciful
One.'" (Bukhari, Muslim)

102. In the *hadith* of ᶜAli ﷺ on the description of how Allah's
Messenger ﷺ used to pray, he reported that at the end of what
he said between the *tashahhud* and the *taslim* was:

اَللَّهُمَّ اغْفِرْلِي مَا قَدَّمْتُ وَمَا أَخَّرْتُ ، وَمَا أَسْرَرْتُ وَمَا
أَعْلَنْتُ ، وَمَا أَسْرَفْتُ وَمَا أَنْتَ أَعْلَمُ بِهِ مِنِّي ، أَنْتَ الْمُقَدِّمُ
وَأَنْتَ الْمُؤَخِّرُ ، لاَ إِلَهَ إِلاَّ أَنْتَ

"O Allah, forgive me my past and future [wrong actions], what
I keep secret and what I make public, what I am extravagant in,
and what You know better than I. You are He who Brings
Forward and He who Puts Back. There is no god but You."
(Muslim)

103. In the *Sunan* of Abu Dawud it is reported that the Prophet
ﷺ enquired of a man, "What do you say in the prayer?" The
man replied, "I recite *tashahhud*, then say:

اَللَّهُمَّ إِنِّي أَسْأَلُكَ الْجَنَّةَ ، وَأَعُوذُ بِكَ مِنَ النَّارِ

'O Allah, I ask You for the Garden and I seek refuge in You ٢.٢. Good
from the Fire,'

though I don't know very well what you pray in a low voice* nor
what Muᶜadh prays in a low voice*."
The Prophet ﷺ said, "We also pray in a low voice* about these
(the Garden and the Fire)." (* دَنْدَنَةٌ lit. the buzzing of bees.)

104. Shaddad ibn Aws ﷺ reported that Allah's Messenger ﷺ
used to say in his prayer:

اَللَّهُمَّ إِنِّي أَسْأَلُكَ الثَّبَاتَ فِي الأَمْرِ ، وَالْعَزِيمَةَ عَلَى الرُّشْدِ ، وَأَسْأَلُكَ شُكْرَ نِعْمَتِكَ ، وَحُسْنَ عِبَادَتِكَ ، وَأَسْأَلُكَ قَلْبًا سَلِيمًا ، وَلِسَانًا صَادِقًا ، وَ أَسْأَلُكَ مِنْ خَيْرِ مَا تَعْلَمُ ، وَأَعُوذُ بِكَ مِنْ شَرِّ مَا تَعْلَمُ ، وَأَسْتَغْفِرُكَ لِمَا تَعْلَمُ ، إِنَّكَ أَنْتَ عَلَّامُ الْغُيُوبِ

"O Allah, I ask You for steadfastness in carrying out what I am commanded, and resolution in taking the right way. I ask You to make me grateful for Your favour and [to enable me] to worship You acceptably. I ask You for a sound heart and a truthful tongue. I ask You for some of the good of what You know. I seek refuge in You from the mischief of what You know. I ask Your forgiveness for what You know. Surely You are the One who is All-knowing of the unseen matters." (An-Nasa'i, at-Tirmidhi)

105. ʿAta' ibn as-Sa'ib told that his father said: ʿAmmar ibn Yasir ؓ led us in a prayer and was brief. One of the people said to him, "You lightened the prayer," or "You made the prayer brief." He replied, "What about that? [Though it was brief] I supplicated with some supplications I heard from Allah's Messenger ﷺ." When he got up to depart one of the people followed him and asked him about the supplication, so he said:

اَللَّهُمَّ بِعِلْمِكَ الْغَيْبَ وَقُدْرَتِكَ عَلَى الْخَلْقِ ، أَحْيِنِي مَا عَلِمْتَ الْحَيَاةَ خَيْرًا لِي ، وَتَوَفَّنِي إِذَا عَلِمْتَ الْوَفَاةَ خَيْرًا لِي ، اَللَّهُمَّ إِنِّي أَسْأَلُكَ خَشْيَتَكَ فِي الْغَيْبِ وَالشَّهَادَةِ ، وَ أَسْأَلُكَ كَلِمَةَ الْحَقِّ فِي الرِّضَا وَالْغَضَبِ ، وَ أَسْأَلُكَ الْقَصْدَ فِي الْفَقْرِ وَالْغِنَى ، وَأَسْأَلُكَ نَعِيمًا لاَ يَنْفَدُ ، وَ أَسْأَلُكَ قُرَّةَ عَيْنٍ لاَ تَنْقَطِعُ ، وَأَسْأَلُكَ الرِّضَا بَعْدَ الْقَضَاءِ ، وَأَسْأَلُكَ بَرْدَ الْعَيْشِ بَعْدَ الْمَوْتِ ، وَأَسْأَلُكَ لَذَّةَ النَّظَرِ إِلَى وَجْهِكَ ،

وَالشَّوْقِ إِلَى لِقَائِكَ فِي غَيْرِ ضَرَّاءَ مُضِرَّةٍ ، وَلاَ فِتْنَةٍ
مُضِلَّةٍ ، اَللَّهُمَّ زَيِّنَّا بِزِينَةِ الإِيمَانِ ، وَاجْعَلْنَا هُدَاةً مُهْتَدِينَ

"O Allah, by Your knowledge of the unseen and Your power over creation, grant me life as long as You know life to be best for me, and take me when You know death to be best for me; O Allah, I ask You for fear of You both in secret and in public; I ask You to enable me to say the truth in pleasure and anger; I ask You for moderation both in poverty and prosperity; I ask You for everlasting bliss; I ask You for uninterrupted happiness; I ask You for contentment after [Your] decree; and I ask You for well-being after death; I ask You for the sweetness of gazing on Your face, and for the longing to meet You, not in harmful distress nor in a trial which leads astray. O Allah, beautify us with the adornment of faith, and make us guides who are rightly guided." (An-Nasa'i)

106. Thawban ؓ said that when Allah's Messenger ﷺ finished his prayer he asked for forgiveness three times and said:

اَللَّهُمَّ أَنْتَ السَّلاَمُ ، وَمِنْكَ السَّلاَمُ ، تَبَارَكْتَ يَا ذَا الْجَلاَلِ
وَالإِكْرَامِ

"O Allah, You are Peace and Peace comes from You. Blessed are You, O Possessor of majesty and honour." (Muslim)

107. Al-Mughirah ibn Shuʿbah ؓ stated that Allah's Messenger ﷺ used to say after he had finished the prayer:

لاَ إِلَهَ إِلاَّ اللَّهُ وَحْدَهُ لاَ شَرِيكَ لَهُ ، لَهُ الْمُلْكُ ، وَلَهُ الْحَمْدُ ،
وَهُوَ عَلَى كُلِّ شَيْءٍ قَدِيرٌ" ، اَللَّهُمَّ لاَ مَانِعَ لِمَا أَعْطَيْتَ ، وَلاَ
مُعْطِيَ لِمَا مَنَعْتَ ، وَلاَ يَنْفَعُ ذَا الْجَدِّ مِنْكَ الْجَدُّ

"There is no god but Allah alone without partner. To Him belongs the kingdom, and to Him praise is due, and He has *power over every thing. O Allah, no one can withhold what You give, or give what You withhold, and riches cannot avail a wealthy person with You."* (Bukhari, Muslim)

108. ʿAbdullah ibn az-Zubayr ؓ at the end of his prayer used to say after the *salam*:

لاَ إِلَهَ إِلاَّ اللَّهُ وَحْدَهُ لاَ شَرِيكَ لَهُ ، لَهُ الْمُلْكُ ، وَلَهُ الْحَمْدُ ،
وَهُوَ عَلَى كُلِّ شَيْءٍ قَدِيرٌ ، وَلاَ حَوْلَ وَلاَ قُوَّةَ إِلاَّ بِاللَّهِ ، لاَ
إِلَهَ إِلاَّ اللَّهُ ، وَلاَ نَعْبُدُ إِلاَّ إِيَّاهُ ، وَلَهُ النِّعْمَةُ ، وَلَهُ الْفَضْلُ ،
وَلَهُ الثَّنَاءُ الْحَسَنُ ، لاَ إِلَهَ إِلاَّ اللَّهُ مُخْلِصِينَ لَهُ الدِّينَ وَلَوْ
كَرِهَ الْكَافِرُونَ

"There is no god but Allah alone who has no partner. To Him belongs the kingdom, to Him praise is due, and He has power over all things. There is no might or power except by Allah. There is no god but Allah whom alone we worship. To Him belongs wealth, to Him belongs grace, and to Him is worthy praise accorded. There is no god but Allah, [we are] sincere to Him regarding the din, even though the disbelievers should disapprove.'"

Ibn az-Zubayr ؓ said, "The Messenger of Allah ﷺ used to declare that there is no god but Allah with this at the end of every prayer." (Muslim)

109. Abu Hurairah ؓ told that the poor emigrants (*Muhajirun*) came to Allah's Messenger ﷺ and said, "The possessors of great wealth have obtained all the highest grades and everlasting bliss. They pray as we do, they fast as we do, they have an excess of wealth with which they perform *Hajj* and ʿ*Umrah*, they go on *jihad* and pay their zakah (sadaqah)." So Allah's Messenger ﷺ said, "Shall I not teach you something by which you will catch up on those who have preceded you and get ahead of those who come

after you, with no-one being better than you except those who do as you do?" They replied, "Certainly, Messenger of Allah." He said, "Glorify [Allah], praise, and declare [His] greatness, thirty-three times after every prayer."

Abu Salih said, "One says:

سُبْحَانَ اللَّهِ ، وَالْحَمْدُ لِلَّهِ ، وَاللَّهُ أَكْبَرُ

'Glory be to Allah, the praise belongs to Allah, and Allah is most great,'

until each one is thirty-three times." (Bukhari, Muslim)

110. Abu Hurairah ؓ also reported Allah's Messenger ﷺ as saying, "If anyone glorifies Allah after every prayer thirty-three times, and praises Allah thirty-three times, and declares Allah is most great thirty-three times, and says to complete the hundred:

لاَ إِلَهَ إِلاَّ اللَّهُ وَحْدَهُ لاَ شَرِيكَ لَهُ ، لَهُ الْمُلْكُ ، وَلَهُ الْحَمْدُ ،
وَهُوَ عَلَى كُلِّ شَيْءٍ قَدِيرٌ

'There is no god but Allah alone without partner; to Him belongs the kingdom, to Him praise is due, and He has power over every thing,'

his wrong actions will be forgiven, even if they are as abundant as the foam of the sea." (Muslim)

111. ᶜAbdullah ibn ᶜAmr ؓ reported that the Prophet ﷺ said: "There are two characteristics which no Muslim slave [of Allah] perseveres in without his entering the Garden. They are easy, and those who act upon them are few. One glorifies Allah ten times after every prayer, praises Him ten times, and declares Him most great ten times. That is a hundred and fifty (with all five prayers) on the tongue, and one thousand five hundred in the scale.

"When one goes to his bed he should declare [Allah] most great thirty-four times, praise [Him] thirty-three times, glorify [Him] thirty-three times, and that is a hundred on the tongue, and a thousand in the scale." He said: I saw Allah's Messenger ﷺ counting them on his hand. They asked, "Messenger of Allah, how are these two things easy and [yet] those who do them are few?" He said, "Shaytan comes to one of you and makes him sleep before he has prayed them, and he comes to him while he is engaged in prayer, reminding him of his needs before he can say them." (Abu Dawud, at-Tirmidhi, and an-Nasa'i)

112. ʿUqbah ibn ʿAmir ؓ said: Allah's Messenger ﷺ told me to recite al-Muʿawwidhat (the two last surahs) after every prayer. (Abu Dawud, at-Tirmidhi, an-Nasa'i)

113. Abu Umamah ؓ said: Allah's Messenger ﷺ was asked, "Which supplication is most readily answered?" He replied, "[That which is asked] in the latter part of the depth of the night and after each of the prescribed prayers." (At-Tirmidhi transmitted it, saying, "It is a hasan hadith.")

114. Muʿadh ibn Jabal ؓ said that Allah's Messenger ﷺ took him by the hand and said, "Muʿadh, by Allah, I love you! Do not fail to say at the end of every prayer:

اَللَّهُمَّ أَعِنِّي عَلَى ذِكْرِكَ ، وَشُكْرِكَ ، وَحُسْنِ عِبَادَتِكَ

'My Lord, help me to remember You, to be grateful to You, and to worship You well." (Abu Dawud and an-Nasa'i)

16. On istikharah (seeking Allah's guidance in a matter)

115. Jabir ibn ʿAbdullah ؓ said: Allah's Messenger ﷺ used to teach us how to ask Allah's guidance [in a matter] just as he used to teach us a surah of the Qur'an, saying, "When any of you intends to do something he should pray two rakʿahs apart from the obligatory prayers. Then let him say:

اَللَّهُمَّ إِنِّي أَسْتَخِيرُكَ بِعِلْمِكَ ، وَأَسْتَقْدِرُكَ بِقُدْرَتِكَ ،
وَأَسْأَلُكَ مِنْ فَضْلِكَ الْعَظِيمِ ، فَإِنَّكَ تَقْدِرُ وَلَا أَقْدِرُ ، وَتَعْلَمُ
وَلَا أَعْلَمُ ، وَأَنْتَ عَلَّامُ الْغُيُوبِ ، اَللَّهُمَّ إِنْ كُنْتَ تَعْلَمُ أَنَّ هٰذَا
الْأَمْرَ - وَتُسَمِّيهِ بِاسْمِهِ - خَيْرٌ لِي فِي دِينِي وَمَعَاشِي
وَعَاقِبَةِ أَمْرِي ، وَعَاجِلِهِ وَآجِلِهِ ، فَاقْدُرْهُ لِي وَيَسِّرْهُ لِي ،
ثُمَّ بَارِكْ لِي فِيهِ ، وَإِنْ كُنْتَ تَعْلَمُ أَنَّ هٰذَا الْأَمْرَ شَرٌّ لِي
فِي دِينِي وَمَعَاشِي وَعَاقِبَةِ أَمْرِي ، وَعَاجِلِهِ وَآجِلِهِ ،
فَاصْرِفْهُ عَنِّي ، وَاصْرِفْنِي عَنْهُ ، وَاقْدُرْ لِي الْخَيْرَ حَيْثُ
كَانَ ثُمَّ رَضِّنِي بِهِ

'O Allah, I ask You [to guide my] choice by Your knowledge, I ask You for strength by Your power, and I ask You of Your great favour, for You have power and I have none, You know and I do not, and You are the One who is Fully Knowing of unseen matters. O Allah, if You know that this matter (and one should name the matter) is good for me regarding my religion, my livelihood, and the outcome of my affair, in its immediate [consequences] and its [the matter's] final term, ordain it for me and make it easy for me, then bless me in it. But if You know that this matter is bad for me regarding my religion, my livelihood, and the outcome of my affair, in its immediate [consequences] and its [the matter's] final term, turn it away from me, turn me away from it, and decree the good for me wherever it is, then make me pleased with it." (Bukhari transmitted it in similar words.)

116. It is mentioned of Anas ﷺ that he said: Allah's Messenger ﷺ said, "Anas when you intend to do something, seek your Lord's [guidance in the] choice seven times, then see what comes first to your heart, because the good is in it."[1]

---

[1] Ibn as-Sunni transmitted it.

The one who (does *istikharah*) supplicates the Creator seeking Him to guide him, and asks the advice of people and is determined in his affairs, will not regret, for Allah, exalted is He, says:

وَشَاوِرْهُمْ فِي الأَمْرِ فَإِذَا عَزَمْتَ فَتَوَكَّلْ عَلَى اللَّه

"And consult with them on the conduct of affairs. And when you are resolved, then put your trust in Allah."

(Qur'an, Al 'Imran: 159)

Qatadah said: A people who seek counsel of each other desiring the face (pleasure) of Allah will be guided to the straightest of their affair.

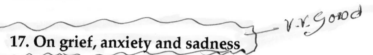

v.v good

17. On grief, anxiety and sadness

117. Ibn ᶜAbbas said that Allah's Messenger used to say when he was distressed:

لاَ إِلَهَ إِلاَّ اللَّهُ الْعَظِيمُ الْحَلِيمُ ، لاَ إِلَهَ إِلاَّ اللَّهُ رَبُّ الْعَرْشِ
الْعَظِيمِ ، لاَ إِلَهَ إِلاَّ اللَّهُ رَبُّ السَّمَوَاتِ وَرَبُّ الأَرْضِ وَرَبُّ
الْعَرْشِ الْكَرِيمِ

"There is no god but Allah, the Incomparably Great, the Forbearing; there is no god but Allah, the Lord of the tremendous Throne; there is no god but Allah, the Lord of the heavens, the Lord of the earth, and the Lord of the noble Throne." (Bukhari, Muslim)

118. Anas said that when anything caused grief to the Prophet he would say:

يَا حَيُّ يَا قَيُّومُ بِرَحْمَتِكَ أَسْتَغِيثُ

"O Living One, O Self-existent One, by Your mercy I seek help." (At-Tirmidhi)

58

119. Abu Hurairah ﷺ reported from the Prophet ﷺ that when something caused him much concern he would raise his head to the sky and say:

$$سُبْحَانَ اللَّهِ الْعَظِيمِ$$

✳ *"Glory be to Allah, the Incomparably Great,"*

and when he exerted himself in supplication he would say:

$$يَا حَيُّ يَا قَيُّومُ$$

✳ *"O Living One, O Self-existent One."* (At-Tirmidhi)

120. Abu Bakrah ﷺ reported Allah's Messenger ﷺ as saying, "The supplications to be used by one who is distressed are:

$$اَللَّهُمَّ رَحْمَتَكَ أَرْجُو ، فَلاَ تَكِلْنِي إِلَى نَفْسِي طَرْفَةَ عَيْنٍ ،$$
$$وَأَصْلِحْ لِي شَأْنِي كُلَّهُ ، لاَ إِلَهَ إِلاَّ أَنْتَ$$

'O Allah, Your mercy is what I hope for. Do not entrust me to myself for the glance of an eye, but put all my affairs in good order for me. There is no god but You.'" (Abu Dawud)

121. Asma' bint ʿUmays ﷺ said: Allah's Messenger ﷺ said to me, "Shall I not teach you phrases which you should say in distress?":

$$اللَّهُ ، اللَّهُ رَبِّي لاَ أُشْرِكُ بِهِ شَيْئًا$$

"Allah, Allah is my Lord, I do not associate anything as partner with Him."

In another version it [is narrated that it] should be said seven times. (Abu Dawud transmitted both versions.)

122. Saʿd ibn Abi Waqqas ﷺ said: Allah's Messenger ﷺ said, "The supplication of Dhu'n-Nun (Yunus) while he was inside the belly of the whale was:

لاَ إِلَهَ إِلاَّ أَنْتَ سُبْحَانَكَ إِنِّي كُنْتُ مِنَ الظَّالِمِينَ

'There is no god but You alone, Glory be to You, surely I was one of the wrongdoers.'"

(Qur'an, al-Anbiya': 87)

He said, "Whenever a Muslim man asks Allah for something with them, Allah will certainly answer him." (At-Tirmidhi)

In another narration, "I know a word which whenever a person in distress says it, Allah will give him relief, that is the word of my brother Yunus ﷺ."[1]

123. Ibn Mas'ud ﷺ reported that Allah's Messenger ﷺ said: "If anyone is afflicted by much care or grief and says:

اَللَّهُمَّ إِنِّي عَبْدُكَ وَابْنُ عَبْدِكَ وَابْنُ أَمَتِكَ ، نَاصِيَتِي بِيَدِكَ ، مَاضٍ فِيَّ حُكْمُكَ ، عَدْلٌ فِيَّ قَضَاؤُكَ ، أَسْأَلُكَ بِكُلِّ اسْمٍ هُوَ لَكَ سَمَّيْتَ بِهِ نَفْسَكَ أَوْ أَنْزَلْتَهُ فِي كِتَابِكَ أَوْ عَلَّمْتَهُ أَحَدًا مِنْ خَلْقِكَ ، أَوِ اسْتَأْثَرْتَ بِهِ فِي عِلْمِ الْغَيْبِ عِنْدَكَ ، أَنْ تَجْعَلَ الْقُرْآنَ رَبِيعَ قَلْبِي ، وَنُورَ صَدْرِي ، وَجَلاَءَ حُزْنِي ، وَذَهَابَ هَمِّي

"O Allah, I am Your slave, the son of Your slave, the son of Your handmaid; my forelock is in Your hand; Your judgement is effected regarding me; Your decree concerning me is just; I ask You by every name which You have and by which You have named Yourself, or sent down in Your Book, or taught any of Your creatures, or kept to Yourself in the knowledge of the unseen, to make the Qur'an a source of delight to my heart, the light of my breast, and the means of clearing away my care and grief,'

then Allah will remove his care and grief and give him joy instead of it." (Ahmad transmitted it in his *Musnad* and Ibn Hibban in his *Sahih*.)

---

[1] Ibn as-Sunni transmitted it with a weak *isnad*.

60

18. On meeting the enemy or a powerful person

124. Abu Musa al-Ash'ari ؓ said that when the Prophet ﷺ feared a people he would say:

اَللَّهُمَّ إِنَّا نَجْعَلُكَ فِي نُحُورِهِمْ ، وَنَعُوذُ بِكَ مِنْ شُرُورِهِمْ

"O Allah, we put You in front of them, and we seek refuge with You from their evils." (Abu Dawud, an-Nasa'i)

125. It is mentioned that when the Prophet ﷺ met the enemy he said:

اَللَّهُمَّ أَنْتَ عَضُدِي ، وَأَنْتَ نَصِيرِي ، بِكَ أَجُولُ ، وَبِكَ أَصُولُ ، وَبِكَ أَقَاتِلُ

"O Allah, You are my aid and You are my helper; by You I move, by You I attack, and by You I fight."[1]

126. The Prophet ﷺ was on an expedition, and he said:

يَا مَالِكَ يَوْمِ الدِّينِ ، إِيَّاكَ نَعْبُدُ ، وَإِيَّاكَ نَسْتَعِينُ

"O Master of the Day of Judgement, You only we worship and You only we ask for help."

Anas said, "I saw men being overthrown, angels striking them from in front of them and from behind."[2]

127. Ibn 'Umar ؓ said: The Messenger of Allah ﷺ said: "When you are afraid of a ruler or someone else, say:

لَا إِلَهَ إِلَّا اللَّهُ الْحَكِيمُ الْكَرِيمُ ، سُبْحَانَ اللَّهِ رَبِّ السَّمَوَاتِ

---

[1] Abu Dawud transmitted it from Anas with a sound isnad.

[2] It is a weak hadith; Ibn as-Sunni transmitted it.

61

VV Good

"There is no god but Allah, the Wise, the Generous. Glory be to Allah, Lord of the seven heavens and Lord of the magnificent throne. There is no god but You. Honoured is the one who is in refuge with You, and great is Your praise. [And there is no god other than You]."[1]

128. ᶜAbdullah ibn ᶜAbbas ﷺ said:

حَسْبُنَا اللَّهُ وَنِعْمَ الْوَكِيلُ

"'Allah is sufficient for us! Most excellent is He in whom we trust,'

(Qur'an, Al ᶜImran: 173)

Ibrahim said it when he was thrown in the fire and Muhammad said it, when people said to him:

إِنَّ النَّاسَ قَدْ جَمَعُوا لَكُمْ

"The people have gathered against you."

(Qur'an, Al ᶜImran: 173)

19. When the shaytan disturbs the child of Adam

Allah, exalted is He, says:

وَقُلْ رَبِّ أَعُوذُ بِكَ مِنْ هَمَزَاتِ الشَّيَاطِينِ ، وَأَعُوذُ بِكَ رَبِّ
أَنْ يَحْضُرُونِ

"And say, 'My Lord! I seek refuge with You from the suggestions of the Shaytans, and I seek refuge with You, my Lord, lest they attend me.'"

(Qur'an, al-Mu'minun: 97-98)

---

[1] Ibn as-Sunni transmitted it with a very weak *isnad*.

129. In the *hadith* of Abu Saʿid al-Khudri ﷺ it is related that the Prophet ﷺ used to say:

أَعُـوذُ بِاللَّهِ مِنَ الشَّـيْـطَانِ الرَّجِـيمِ ، مِـنْ نَفْـخِـهِ وَنَفْـثِـهِ وَهَمْزِهِ

"'I seek refuge with Allah from the accursed Shaytan, from his puffing up (nafkh), his spitting (nafth), and his evil suggestion (hamz),' (See also hadith 79.)

because of the words of Allah, exalted is He:

وَإِمَّا يَنْزَغَنَّكَ مِنَ الشَّـيْطَانِ نَزْغٌ فَاسْتَـعِذْ بِاللَّهِ إِنَّهُ هُوَ السَّمِيعُ الْعَلِيمُ

'And if an incitement from the Shaytan reaches you then seek refuge in Allah. Truly, He is the Hearer, the Knower.'"

(Qur'an, Fussilat: 36) (At-Tirmidhi, Abu Dawud and an-Nasa'i)

The *Adhan* repels the Shaytan:

130. The Prophet ﷺ said, "When the call to prayer is made, the Shaytan turns his back and breaks wind, but when the call is finished he turns around. When a second call to prayer (the *iqamah*) is made he turns his back, and when the second call is finished he turns around [to distract one]." (Bukhari, Muslim)

131. Suhail ibn Abi Salih said: My father sent me to Banu Harithah and along with me a servant or a companion. Someone called him by name from an enclosure. The person with me looked over the wall, but saw nothing. I mentioned that to my father. He said, "If I had known that you would meet such a situation I would never have sent you [there], but [bear in mind] whenever you hear such a call [from the jinn] call the *adhan*, for I have heard Abu Hurairah relating that the Messenger of Allah ﷺ said: 'Whenever the

adhan is called for the prayer, the Shaytan runs back.'" (Muslim)

132. Zayd ibn Aslam reported that he was put in charge of Maᶜadin. They mentioned to him the abundance of jinn there. He told them to call the *adhan* at all times and very often. After that, they did not see anything. (i.e. there were no jinn left in the area).

133. Abu ad-Darda' said: Allah's Messenger ﷺ stood up [to pray] and we heard him say:

أَعُوذُ بِاللَّهِ مِنْكَ

✳ *"I seek refuge in Allah from you."*
and then he said:

أَلْعَنُكَ بِلَعْنَةِ اللَّهِ

✳ *"I curse you with Allah's curse"*
three times, then he stretched out his hand as though he was taking hold of something. When he finished the prayer, we said, "Messenger of Allah, we heard you say something during the prayer which we have not heard you say before, and we saw you stretch out your hand." He replied, "Allah's enemy Iblis came with a brand of fire to put it in my face, so I said three times: "I seek refuge in Allah from you." Then I said three times: "I curse you with Allah's full curse." But he did not retreat. Then I wanted to seize him. By Allah! Had it not been for the supplication of my brother Sulayman, he would have been bound, and the children of the people of Madinah would have played with him." (Muslim)

134. ᶜUthman ibn Abi'l-ᶜAs ﷺ said: I said, "Messenger of Allah, the Shaytan came between me and my prayer and my recitation of Qur'an, causing confusion in my mind." He ﷺ replied, "That is a shaytan called Khanzab; so when you feel his presence seek refuge with Allah from him and spit three times on your left side." ᶜUthman said: I did so and Allah drove him away from me. (Muslim)

135. Abu Zumail said: I said to Ibn ʿAbbas ﷺ: "What is that thing I find in my self?" meaning doubt. He said, "If you find something in your heart, say:

هُوَ الأَوَّلُ وَالآخِرُ وَالظَّاهِرُ وَالْبَاطِنُ ، وَهُوَ بِكُلِّ شَيْءٍ عَلِيمٌ

"He is the First and the Last, the Outward and the Inward; and He knows fully all things."

(Qur'an, al-Hadid: 3) (Abu Dawud)

20. On submitting to fate

Allah says, exalted is He:

يَا أَيُّهَا الَّذِينَ آمَنُوا لاَ تَكُونُوا كَالَّذِينَ كَفَرُوا وَقَالُوا لإِخْوَانِهِمْ إِذَا ضَرَبُوا فِي الأَرْضِ أَوْ كَانُوا غُزًّا لَوْ كَانُوا عِنْدَنَا مَا مَاتُوا وَمَا قُتِلُوا لِيَجْعَلَ اللَّهُ ذَٰلِكَ حَسْرَةً فِي قُلُوبِهِمْ وَاللَّهُ يُحْيِي وَيُمِيتُ وَاللَّهُ بِمَا تَعْمَلُونَ بَصِيرٌ

"O you who believe! Do not be as those who disbelieved and said of their brethren who went abroad in the land or were fighting in the field, 'If they had been [here] with us they would not have died and would not have been killed;' that Allah may make it anguish in their hearts. Allah gives life and causes death; and Allah is Seer of what you do."

(Qur'an, Al ʿImran: 156)

136. Abu Hurairah ﷺ said: Allah's Messenger ﷺ said, "The strong believer is better and more beloved to Allah, exalted is He, than the weak believer, and in each there is good. Cherish that which gives you benefit and seek help from Allah, mighty is He and majestic, and do not lose heart. And if anything (trouble) happens to you, don't say, 'If only I had done [that], it would

have been such and such,' but say:

$$\text{قَدَّرَ اللَّهُ وَمَا شَاءَ فَعَلَ}$$

'Allah decreed, and that which He willed, He did,'
for 'if' opens [the door] for the Shaytan." (Muslim)

137. ʿAwf ibn Malik related that the Prophet gave a decision between two men, and the one against whom the decision was given said as he turned away, "Allah is sufficient for me! Most excellent is He in whom I trust." The Prophet said, "Allah reproaches [one] for incapacity, but be intelligent, and when a matter gets the better of you, say:

$$\text{حَسْبِيَ اللَّهُ وَنِعْمَ الْوَكِيلُ}$$

'Allah is sufficient for me! Most excellent is He in whom I trust.'" (Abu Dawud)

21. What one should say on receiving a blessing or bounty

Allah, exalted is He, says:

$$\text{وَلَوْ لاَ إِذْ دَخَلْتَ جَنَّتَكَ قُلْتَ مَا شَاءَ اللَّهُ لاَ قُوَّةَ إِلاَّ بِاللَّهِ}$$

"If only, when you entered your garden, you had said, 'That which Allah wills [will come to pass]! There is no strength save in Allah.'"
(Qur'an, al-Kahf: 39)

138. Anas ibn Malik said: Allah's Messenger said, "If Allah bestows a bounty on a slave in his family, property and offspring, and he says:

$$\text{مَا شَاءَ اللَّهُ لاَ قُوَّةَ إِلاَّ بِاللَّهِ}$$

'That which Allah wills [will come to pass]! There is no strength save in Allah,' then he will never see in them any affliction except for death [when the time comes]."[1]

139. The Prophet ﷺ when he saw anything which pleased him, would say:

الْحَمْدُ لِلَّهِ الَّذِي بِنِعْمَتِهِ تَتِمُّ الصَّالِحَاتُ

"Praise belongs to Allah through whose blessing righteous actions are accomplished,"
and when he saw anything which displeased him, he would say:

الْحَمْدُ لِلَّهِ عَلَى كُلِّ حَالٍ

"Praise be to Allah in all states."[2]

22. On the believer being afflicted with a major or minor misfortune

Allah, exalted is He, says:

اَلَّذِينَ إِذَا أَصَابَتْهُمْ مُصِيبَةٌ قَالُوا إِنَّا لِلَّهِ وَإِنَّا إِلَيْهِ رَاجِعُونَ ، أُولَئِكَ عَلَيْهِمْ صَلَوَاتٌ مِنْ رَبِّهِمْ وَرَحْمَةٌ وَ أُولَئِكَ هُمُ الْمُهْتَدُونَ

"Who say, when a misfortune strikes them, 'Truly, we are Allah's and truly, to Him we are returning.' Those are they on whom are blessings from their Lord and mercy. Those are the rightly guided."
(Qur'an, al-Baqarah: 156-7)

140. It is mentioned of Abu Hurairah ﵁ that he said: Allah's Messenger ﷺ said, "Each of you should say:

---

[1] At-Tabarani transmitted it. It is a weak *hadith*.

[2] Ibn Majah. Al-Hakim and others regard it as having a *sahih isnad*.

إِنَّا لِلَّهِ وَإِنَّا إِلَيْهِ رَاجِعُونَ

'Truly, we are Allah's and truly, to Him we are returning'
for everything, even for the [breaking of the] thong of his sandals,
because it is one of the afflictions."[1]

141. Umm Salamah ڤ said: I heard Allah's Messenger ﷺ
saying, "If any slave to whom a misfortune occurs then says:

إِنَّا لِلَّهِ وَإِنَّا إِلَيْهِ رَاجِعُونَ ، اَللَّهُمَّ أَجُرْنِي فِي مُصِيبَتِي
وَأَخْلِفْ لِي خَيْرًا مِنْهَا

'Truly, we are Allah's and truly, to Him we are returning;
O Allah, reward me for my misfortune and give me something
better than it in exchange.'

Allah will reward him for his misfortune and give him something
better than it in exchange."

When Abu Salamah died, I said as the Messenger of Allah ﷺ
had told me to, and Allah gave me better than him: the Messenger
of Allah ﷺ. (Muslim)

142. She said: Allah's Messenger ﷺ came to Abu Salamah when
his eyes were fixedly open. He closed them and then he said,
"When the spirit is taken the sight follows it." Some of his family
wept and wailed, so he said, "Do not supplicate for yourselves
anything but good, for the angels say *'Amin'* to what you say."
He then said:

اَللَّهُمَّ اغْفِرْ لِأَبِي سَلَمَةَ ، وَارْفَعْ دَرَجَتَهُ فِي الْمَهْدِيِّينَ ،
وَاخْلُفْهُ فِي عَقِبِهِ فِي الْغَابِرِينَ ، وَاغْفِرْ لَنَا وَلَهُ يَا رَبَّ
الْعَالَمِينَ ، وَافْسَحْ لَهُ فِي قَبْرِهِ وَنَوِّرْ لَهُ فِيهِ

"O Allah, forgive Abu Salamah, raise his degree among those
who are rightly guided, and grant him a succession in his

---

[1] A *hasan hadith.*

68

descendants who remain. Forgive both us and him, Lord of the worlds, make his grave spacious for him and grant him light in it." (Muslim)

23. On debt

143. ᶜAli ؓ said that a slave, who had made a contract with his master to pay for his freedom, came to him and said, "I am unable to fulfil my contract, so help me." He said, "Shall I not teach you some words which Allah's Messenger ﷺ taught me, and which even if you had a debt as large as a mountain Allah would pay it for you?":

$$ اَللَّهُمَّ اكْفِنِي بِحَلَالِكَ عَنْ حَرَامِكَ ، وَأَغْنِنِي بِفَضْلِكَ عَمَّنْ سِوَاكَ $$

"O Allah, grant me enough of what You make lawful that I may dispense with what You make unlawful, and make me independent, by Your bounty, of other than You." (At-Tirmidhi narrated it saying, "It is a *hasan hadith*.")

24. On incantations and charms

144. Abu Saᶜid al-Khudri ؓ said: A group of Companions of the Prophet ﷺ set out on a journey until they reached a certain Arab tribe. They requested hospitality but they refused. The leader of that tribe was stung [by a scorpion]. They tried everything on him but nothing availed. One of the tribesmen said, "Why not go to these people who have just settled? Perhaps one of them may have something." They came to them and said, "O people! Our chief has been stung and we have tried everything but nothing worked. Can any of you do something?"

One of the Companions said, "Yes, by Allah! I practise incantation. However, by Allah, we requested hospitality from you and you refused. So I will not practise incantation on your leader until you

69

pay us." They made an agreement for a flock of sheep. The Companion started spitting on him (the leader) and reciting Surah al-Fatihah. And it was as though he had been set free after being hobbled [like a camel]. The man stood and began walking, free of any pain.

They paid them their price which they had agreed with them. One of them [the Companions] said, "Divide them up." The one who had performed the incantation said, "Let us not do it until we go to the Messenger of Allah ﷺ and mention to him what happened [and see what he tells us to do]." They went to the Messenger of Allah ﷺ and mentioned it to him. He said, "And what makes you think that it (the Fatihah) is an incantation?" Then he said, "You are right, divide it (i.e. the flock of sheep) and give me a share of it." Then the Prophet ﷺ laughed. (Bukhari, Muslim)

145. Ibn ʿAbbas ﷺ said that Allah's Messenger ﷺ used to seek [Allah's] protection for al-Hasan and al-Husain, saying:

أُعِيـذُكُمَا بِكَلِمَاتِ اللَّهِ الـتَّامَّـةِ مِنْ كُلِّ شَـيْطَانٍ وَهَامَّـةٍ ،
وَمِنْ كُلِّ عَيْنٍ لَأَمَّةٍ

"I seek protection for the two of you with Allah's perfect words from every Shaytan and poisonous creature and from every evil eye."

And he would say, "Your ancestor [Ibrahim] used to seek protection with them for Ismaʿil and Ishaq." (Bukhari)

146. ʿA'ishah ﷺ said that when a person complained of some trouble, or if he had a sore or a wound, the Prophet ﷺ would say, while with his finger just so,

([while narrating this *hadith*] Sufyan ibn ʿUyaynah put his finger on the earth then raised it):

بِسْمِ اللَّهِ تُرْبَةُ أَرْضِنَا بِرِيقَةِ بَعْضِنَا يُشْفَى سَقِيمُنَا بِإِذْنِ
رَبِّنَا

✳ *"In the name of Allah. It is the soil of our land with the spittle of one of us, that our sick one may be healed by our Lord's permission."* (Bukhari, Muslim)

147. ᶜA'ishah said that the Prophet used to seek protection for anyone of his family by wiping him with his right hand and then saying:

اَللّٰهُمَّ رَبَّ النَّاسِ ، أَذْهِبِ الْبَأْسَ ، وَاشْفِ أَنْتَ الشَّافِي ، لاَ شِفَاءَ إلاَّ شِفَاؤُكَ ، شِفَاءً لاَ يُغَادِرُ سَقَمًا

✳ *"O Allah, Lord of men, remove the harm, and heal, You are the Healer. There is no healing but Yours, a healing which leaves no illness behind."* (Bukhari, Muslim)

148. ᶜUthman ibn Abi'l-ᶜAs said that he complained to Allah's Messenger of a pain he had in his body ever since he had become a Muslim. The Messenger of Allah said: "Put your hand on the part of your body which is sore and say three times:

بِسْمِ اللّٰهِ

✳ *"In the name of Allah,"*
and seven times,

أَعُوذُ بِعِزَّةِ اللّٰهِ وَقُدْرَتِهِ مِنْ شَرِّ مَا أَجِدُ وَأُحَاذِرُ

✳ *"I seek refuge in Allah's might and power from the mischief of what I am experiencing and trying to avert."* (Muslim)

149. Ibn ᶜAbbas reported Allah's Messenger as saying, "No Muslim will visit a sick person, whose time has not come, and say seven times:

أَسْأَلُ اللّٰهَ رَبَّ الْعَرْشِ الْعَظِيمِ أَنْ يَشْفِيَكَ

✳ *"I ask Allah, the Mighty, Lord of the mighty throne, to cure you"*

71

but that he will be cured." (Abu Dawud and at-Tirmidhi transmitted it. At-Tirmidhi said, "It is a *hasan hadith*.")

25. On entering cemeteries

150. Buraidah ﷺ said: Allah's Messenger ﷺ used to teach them to say when they went out to the cemeteries:

الـسَّـلاَمُ عَلَيْكُمْ أَهْلَ الدِّيَارِ مِـنَ الْمُـؤْمـنِينَ وَالْمُـسْلِمِـينَ ،
وَإِنَّـا إِنْ شَـاءَ اللَّهُ بِكُمْ لاَحِـقُـونَ ، نَسْـأَلُ اللَّهَ لَنَا وَلَكُمُ
الْعَافِيَةَ

"Peace be upon you, inhabitants of the dwellings who have believed in Allah and submitted to Him. If Allah wills, we shall join you. We ask Allah for us and for you well-being." (Muslim)

26. On prayer for rain (*istisqa'*)

151. Jabir ibn ᶜAbdullah ﷺ said: Women came to the Prophet ﷺ weeping. The Prophet ﷺ said:

اَللَّهُمَّ اسْقِنَا غَيْثًا مُغِيثًا ، مَرِيئًا مَرِيعًا نَافِعًا غَيْرَ ضَارٍّ ،
عَاجِلاً غَيْرَ آجِلٍ

"O Allah, give us rain which will replenish us, abundant, fertilising and beneficial, not injurious, granting it now, not later."

Thereupon the sky became overcast. (Abu Dawud)

152. ᶜA'ishah ﷺ said: People complained to Allah's Messenger ﷺ of the lack of rain, so he gave orders for a *mimbar* [to be set up for him], and it was set up for him at the *musalla* (place of prayer in the open used for the ᶜId prayers). He appointed a day for the people when they should come out. Allah's Messenger ﷺ came out when the rim of the sun appeared and sat down on the *mimbar* and declared Allah's greatness and praised Him, mighty

and majestic is He. Then he said, "You have complained of drought in your abodes and of delay in receiving rain at the beginning of its season, but Allah, glorious is He, has ordered you to supplicate Him and has promised that He will answer your prayers." Then he said:

الْحَـمْـدُ لِلَّه رَبِّ الْعَـالَـمِينَ الرَّحْـمَنِ الرَّحِـيمِ مَـالك يَـوْمِ
الدِّينِ ، لَا إِلَهَ إِلَّا اللَّهُ يَفْعَلُ مَا يُرِيدُ ، اَللَّهُمَّ أَنْتَ اللَّهُ لَا إِلَهَ
إِلَّا أَنْتَ الْغَـنِيُّ ، وَنَحْـنُ الْـفُـقَـرَاءُ ، أَنْزِلْ عَلَيْنَا الْغَـيْثَ ،
وَاجْعَلْ مَا أَنْزَلْتَ لَنَا قُوَّةً وَبَلَاغًا إِلَى حِينٍ

"Praise be to Allah, the Lord of the universe, the Compassionate, the Merciful, the Master of the day of judgement. There is no god but Allah who does what He wishes. O Allah, You are Allah there is no god but You, the Free of Need, and we are the needy. Send down rain upon us and make what You send down a strength and satisfaction for us for a time."

He then raised his hands and kept raising them till the whiteness under his armpits was visible. He then turned his back to the people and inverted (or, turned round) his cloak while keeping his hands aloft. He then faced the people, descended and prayed two rak'ahs. Allah, mighty and majestic is He, then produced a cloud, and a storm of thunder and lightning broke out. Then it rained by the permission of Allah, exalted is He, and before he reached his mosque streams were flooding. When he saw the speed with which the people sought shelter he laughed ﷺ till his back teeth were visible. Then he said, "I testify that Allah has power over every thing and that I am Allah's slave and Messenger." (Abu Dawud)

27. On the wind

153. Abu Hurairah ﷺ said: I heard Allah's Messenger ﷺ say, "The wind comes from Allah's mercy. It brings mercy and it brings

punishment. When you see it do not revile it. Ask Allah for its good and seek refuge in Him from its mischief." (Abu Dawud, Ibn Majah)

154. ʿAʾishah ﷛ said: The Prophet ﷺ when the wind was stormy, said:

اَللَّهُمَّ إِنِّي أَسْأَلُكَ خَيْرَهَا ، وَخَيْرَ مَا فِيهَا ، وَخَيْرَ مَا أُرْسِلَتْ بِهِ ، وَأَعُوذُ بِكَ مِنْ شَرِّهَا وَشَرِّ مَا فِيهَا ، وَشَرِّ مَا أُرْسِلَتْ بِهِ

"O Allah, I ask You for its good, the good of what is in it and the good of what it was sent for, and I seek refuge in You from its mischief, the mischief of what is in it and the mischief of what it was sent for." (Muslim)

155. ʿAʾishah ﷛ said that when the Prophet ﷺ saw something rising in the sky (meaning clouds), he would leave what he was doing, even if he was in [preparation for] salah, and say:

اَللَّهُمَّ إِنِّي أَعُوذُ بِكَ مِنْ شَرِّهَا

"O Allah, I seek refuge in You from their mischief."
If Allah cleared them away he praised Him, and if rain fell he said:

اَللَّهُمَّ صَيِّبًا هَنِيئًا

"O Allah, [make it] a beneficial downpour." (Abu Dawud, an-Nasaʾi and Ibn Majah)

28. On thunder

156. When ʿAbdullah ibn az-Zubayr ﷛ heard thunder, he stopped talking and said:

سُبْحَانَ الَّذِي يُسَبِّحُ الرَّعْدُ بِحَمْدِهِ ، وَالْمَلاَئِكَةُ مِنْ خِيفَتِهِ

*"Glory be to Him whom the thunder glorifies with His praise
and the angels extol from fear of Him."[1]* ax101 – high, Allah

157. Ka'b said: Whoever says that (the above du'a) three times,
will be saved from that thunder.[2]

158. 'Abdullah ibn 'Umar told that when the Prophet
heard the sound of thunder and of thunderbolts he said:

اَللَّهُمَّ لاَ تَقْتُلْنَا بِغَضَبِكَ ، وَلاَتُهْلِكْنَا بِعَذَابِكَ ، وَعَافِنَا قَبْلَ
ذٰلِكَ

*"O Allah, do not kill us with Your anger and do not destroy us
with Your punishment, but preserve us before that happens."*
(At-Tirmidhi)

29. On raining

159. Zayd ibn Khalid al-Juhani said: The Messenger of Allah
led our morning *salah* at Hudaybiyyah after it had rained during
the previous night. When he turned away [after the prayer] he faced
the people and said, "Do you know what your Lord said?" They
said, "Allah and His Messenger know best." He said, "Allah has
said, 'This morning there are some of My slaves who believe in Me
and some who disbelieve. The one who said, "We have had rain by
the bounty of Allah and His mercy," believes in Me, and rejects the
[power attributed to the] stars; and the one who said, "We have had
rain with the help of such and such stars," denies Me and believes in
the stars'." (Bukhari, Muslim)

---

[1] Malik transmitted it; the *isnad* of this *hadith* is sound.

[2] At-Tabarani narrated it; al-Hafiz (Ibn Hajar) said that its *isnad* is sound.

160. Anas ﷺ said: A man entered the Mosque on a Friday while Allah's Messenger ﷺ was standing delivering the *khutbah*. The man said: "O Allah's Messenger, livestock are dying and the roads are cut off; please ask Allah for rain." So Allah's Messenger ﷺ raised both his hands and said:

اَللَّهُمَّ أَغِثْنَا ، اَللَّهُمَّ أَغِثْنَا

✳ *"O Allah! Give us rain. O Allah! Give us rain."*

Anas added: By Allah, there were no clouds in the sky and there was no house or building between us and the mountain of Sal⁾. Then a big cloud like a shield appeared from behind it and when it was in the middle of the sky, it spread and then rained. By Allah! We could not see the sun for a week. The next Friday, a person entered through the same gate and Allah's Messenger ﷺ was delivering the Friday *khutbah* and the man stood in front of him and said, "O Allah's Messenger, the livestock are dying and the roads are cut off; please invoke Allah to withhold rain." Anas added, "Allah's Messenger ﷺ raised both hands and said:

اَللَّهُمَّ حَوَالِينَا وَلاَ عَلَيْنَا ، اَللَّهُمَّ عَلَى الآكَامِ ، وَالظِّرَابِ ، وَبُطُونِ الأَوْدِيَةِ ، وَمَنَابِتِ الشَّجَرِ

✳ *'O Allah! [Let it rain] around us and not on us. O Allah! On the plateaus, on the mountains, on the hills, in the valleys and on the places where trees grow'."*

Anas added: The rain stopped and we came out, walking in the sun. (Bukhari, Muslim)

30. On seeing the new moon

161. ⁾Abdullah ibn ⁾Umar ﷺ said: When Allah's Messenger ﷺ saw the new moon he used to say:

اللَّهُ أَكْبَرُ ، اَللَّهُمَّ أَهِلَّهُ عَلَيْنَا بِالأَمْنِ وَالإِيمَانِ ، وَالسَّلاَمَةِ

وَالإِسْلاَمِ ، وَالتَّوْفِيقِ لِمَا تُحِبُّ وَتَرْضَى ، رَبُّنَا وَرَبُّكَ اللَّهُ

"Allah is most great, make the new moon rise on us, with security, faith, safety and Islam, and favour us with what You love and what pleases You. My Lord and your Lord is Allah." (Ad-Darimi transmitted it, and also at-Tirmidhi in a slightly shorter version from a *hadith* of Talhah)

31. On fasting and breaking fast

162. Abu Hurairah ؓ said: Allah's Messenger ﷺ said, "There are three whose supplications are not rejected: the fasting man until he breaks his fast, the just Imam (i.e. Khalifah or Amir), and the supplication of the one who has been wronged." (At-Tirmidhi transmitted it, saying, "It is a *hasan hadith*.")

163. Ibn Abi Mulaykah reported that ᶜAbdullah ibn ᶜAmr ؓ, said: I heard Allah's Messenger ﷺ saying, "For the fasting person at the time of breaking his fast there is a supplication which will not be rejected."
Ibn Abi Mulaykah said: I heard ᶜAbdullah ibn ᶜAmr saying when he broke his fast:

اَللَّهُمَّ إِنِّي أَسْأَلُكَ بِرَحْمَتِكَ الَّتِي وَسِعَتْ كُلَّ شَيْءٍ أَنْ تَغْفِرَ لِي

"O Allah, I ask You by Your mercy, which encompasses everything, that You forgive me." (Ibn Majah and others)

164. It is mentioned that when the Prophet ﷺ broke his fast he would say:

اَللَّهُمَّ لَكَ صُمْتُ ، وَعَلَى رِزْقِكَ أَفْطَرْتُ

"O Allah, for You I have fasted and with Your provision I have broken my fast."

77

165. In another version:

اَللَّهُمَّ لَكَ صُمْنَا ، وَعَلَى رِزْقِكَ أَفْطَرْنَا ، فَتَقَبَّلْ مِنَّا إِنَّكَ أَنْتَ السَّمِيعُ الْعَلِيمُ

"O Allah, for You we have fasted and with Your provision we have broken our fasts. So accept [the fast] from us, surely You are the All-Hearing, All-Knowing."[1]

32. On travelling

166. It is mentioned from Allah's Messenger ﷺ that he said, "A man cannot leave behind with his family anything better than two *rak'ahs* which he prays when he intends to travel." (At-Tabarani)

167. Abu Hurairah ؓ related that the Prophet ﷺ said, "Whoever intends to travel should say to the people he leaves behind:

أَسْتَوْدِعُكُمُ اللَّهَ الَّذِي لاَ تَضِيعُ وَدَائِعُهُ

"I entrust you to Allah whose trusts are never neglected."[2]

168. Ibn ʿUmar ؓ related that Allah's Messenger ﷺ said, "Whenever anything is entrusted [to Him], truly Allah will guard it." (Ahmad and others transmitted it)

169. Salim said: Ibn ʿUmar ؓ used to say to a man when he meant to travel, "Come close to me so that I can entrust you [to Allah] as the Messenger of Allah ﷺ used to entrust us [to Allah]." Then he would say:

---

[1] Both versions have weak *isnads*, the latter being weaker.

[2] It is a *hadith* with a *hasan isnad*, transmitted by Ibn Majah, an-Nasa'i, Ahmad and others.

أَسْتَوْدِعُ اللَّهَ دِينَكَ وَأَمَانَتَكَ وَخَوَاتِيمَ عَمَلِكَ

* *"I entrust to Allah your din, what you are responsible for and your life's concluding deeds."*

In another version: He – meaning the Prophet ﷺ – when he bade farewell to a man, would take hold of his hand and not let it go until the man was the one to let go of the hand of the Prophet ﷺ, while praying for him. (At-Tirmidhi said, "This is a *hasan sahih hadith*.")

170. Anas ibn Malik ﷺ said: A man came to the Prophet ﷺ and said, "Messenger of Allah, I intend to go on a journey, so give me provision (i.e. advice)." He replied:

زَوَّدَكَ اللَّهُ التَّقْوَى

* *"May Allah provide you with taqwa (consciousness of Allah)!"*

He said, "Give me more!" so he added:

وَغَفَرَ ذَنْبَكَ

* *"And may He forgive your wrong action."*

He said, "Give me more!" and he added:

وَيَسَّرَ لَكَ الْخَيْرَ حَيْثُمَا كُنْتَ

** *"And may He make that which is good easy for you wherever you are."* (At-Tirmidhi said, "This is a *hasan gharib hadith*.")

171. Abu Hurairah ﷺ told of a man who said, "Messenger of Allah, I intend to make a journey, so advise me." He told him, "Have fear of Allah and say اَللَّهُ أَكْبَرُ 'Allah is most great' on every rising ground," and when the man turned away he said:

اَللَّهُمَّ اطْوِ لَهُ الْبُعْدَ ، وَهَوِّنْ عَلَيْهِ السَّفَرَ

* *"O Allah, make the distance short for him and make the journey easy for him."* (At-Tirmidhi said, "A *hasan hadith*.")

33. On riding an animal

172. ʿAli ibn Rabiʿah said: I witnessed ʿAli ibn Abi Talib ﷺ being brought an animal to ride. When he put his foot in the stirrup he said:

بِسْمِ اللَّهِ

✳ *"In the name of Allah."*

Then when he sat on its back he said:

الْحَمْدُ لِلَّهِ

✳ *"Praise be to Allah."*

He then said:

سُبْحَانَ الَّذِي سَخَّرَ لَنَا هَذَا وَمَا كُنَّا لَهُ مُقْرِنِينَ ، وَإِنَّا إِلَى رَبِّنَا لَمُنْقَلِبُونَ

✳✳✳ **"Glorified be He who subjected this to us, and we were not capable [of subjecting it], and to our Lord we are returning."**

(Qur'an, az-Zukhruf 13-14)

He then said:

الْحَمْدُ لِلَّهِ

✳ *"Praise be to Allah"* three times

and

اللَّهُ أَكْبَرُ

✳ *"Allah is most great"* three times,

and then he said:

سُبْحَانَكَ ، اَللَّهُمَّ إِنِّي ظَلَمْتُ نَفْسِي ، فَاغْفِرْلِي ، فَإِنَّهُ لاَ يَغْفِرُ الذُّنُوبَ إِلاَّ أَنْتَ

✳ "Glory be to You. O Allah, I have wronged myself, so forgive me, for no-one forgives wrong actions but You."

He then laughed. Someone asked, "Amir al-Mu'minin, what are you laughing at?" He replied, "I saw the Prophet ﷺ do as I did and then he laughed. So I said, 'Messenger of Allah, what did you laugh at?' He said, 'Your Lord, glorious and exalted is He, is pleased with His slave when he says, "My Lord forgive me my wrong actions," [for Allah says], "He knows that no-one forgives wrong actions other than Me".'" (Abu Dawud, an-Nasa'i and at-Tirmidhi transmitted it. At-Tirmidhi said, "This is a *hasan sahih hadith*.")

173. Muslim related from ʿAbdullah ibn ʿUmar ؓ that when the Prophet ﷺ sat on his camel ready to go out on a journey, he said:

$$\text{اللَّهُ أَكْبَرُ}$$

✳ "Allah is most great" three times.
Then he said:

$$\text{سُبْحَانَ الَّذِي سَخَّرَ لَنَا هَذَا وَمَا كُنَّا لَهُ مُقْرِنِينَ ، وَإِنَّا إِلَى}$$
$$\text{رَبِّنَا لَمُنْقَلِبُونَ}$$

"Glorified be He who subjected this to us, and we were not capable [of subjecting it], and to our Lord we are returning."

(Qur'an, az-Zukhruf 13-14)

$$\text{اَللَّهُمَّ إِنَّا نَسْأَلُكَ فِي سَفَرِنَا هَذَا الْبِرَّ وَالتَّقْوَى ، وَمِنَ}$$
$$\text{الْعَمَلِ مَا تَرْضَى ، اَللَّهُمَّ هَوِّنْ عَلَيْنَا سَفَرَنَا هَذَا ، وَاطْوِ}$$
$$\text{عَنَّا بُعْدَهُ ، أَنْتَ الصَّاحِبُ فِي السَّفَرِ ، وَالْخَلِيفَةُ فِي}$$
$$\text{الأَهْلِ ، اَللَّهُمَّ إِنِّي أَعُوذُ بِكَ مِنْ وَعْثَاءِ السَّفَرِ ، وَكَآبَةِ}$$
$$\text{الْمَنْظَرِ ، وَسُوءِ الْمُنْقَلَبِ فِي الْمَالِ وَالأَهْلِ}$$

✳ "O Allah, we ask You in this journey of ours for uprightness, taqwa and such deeds as are pleasing to You. O Allah, make

*this journey of ours easy for us and make its length short for us.
You are the Companion in the journey and the Successor and
Guardian of the family. O Allah, I seek refuge with You from
the difficulty of travelling, the bad and undesirable things that I
may see, and from finding that harm has come when I return to
my property and family."*

When he returned he said these words, adding:

آئِبُونَ ، تَائِبُونَ ، عَابِدُونَ ، لِرَبِّنَا حَامِدُونَ

*"[We are] Returning, repentant, worshipping, [and] to our Lord
praising."* (Muslim)

174. In another version: When Allah's Messenger ﷺ and his
Companions topped high ground, they said, اَللَّهُ أَكْــبَرُ "Allah is
most great" and when they descended they said, سُبْحَانَ اللَّه "Glory
be to Allah" (It is in the *sahih*)

34. On a journey by sea

175. It is mentioned from Husain ibn ᶜAli ﷺ that he said: Allah's
Messenger ﷺ said, "It is a security for my community from
drowning that when they board a ship they say:

بِسْمِ اللَّه مَجْرَيهَا وَمُرْسَاهَا ، إِنَّ رَبِّي لَغَفُورٌ رَحِيمٌ

'In the name of Allah be its course and its mooring.
Truly, my Lord is All-Forgiving, Compassionate,'
(Qur'an, Hud: 41)

and:

وَمَا قَدَرُوا اللَّهَ حَقَّ قَدْرِه

'And they do not measure the power of Allah with His
true measure'."
(Qur'an, al-Anᶜam: 92)[1]

---

[1] Ibn as-Sunni and Abu Yaᶜla al-Mawsili transmitted it.

35. On riding a troublesome animal

176. Yunus ibn ʿUbaid, may Allah show mercy to him, said, "If a man was riding a troublesome beast and said in its ear:

أَفَـغَـيْـرَ دِيـنِ اللَّهِ يَبْـغُـونَ وَلَهُ أَسْلَمَ مَنْ فِي السَّمَـوَاتِ
وَالأَرْضِ طَوْعًا وَكَرْهًا وَإِلَيْهِ يُرْجَعُونَ

'Do they seek other than the religion of Allah, when to Him submits whosoever is in the heavens and the earth, willingly, or unwillingly, and to Him they will be returned,'

(Qur'an, Al ʿImran: 83)

then it would stop by the leave of Allah, exalted is He."
"We did this and so it happened by the permission of Allah, exalted is He."

36. On the animal when it runs away in the wilderness

177. Ibn Masʿud related that the Prophet said, "If an animal of any one of you runs away from him in the wilderness then let him shout:

يَا عِبَادَ اللَّهِ احْبِسُوا ، يَا عِبَادَ اللَّهِ احْبِسُوا

'O slaves of Allah, stop it. O slaves of Allah, stop it,'

because Allah, mighty and majestic is He, has in the land an attendant who will stop it."[1]

37. On intending to enter a village or a city

178. It is related from Suhaib that the Prophet never caught sight of a town he proposed to enter without immediately uttering the following words:

---

[1] At-Tabarani and Ibn as-Sunni transmitted this *hadith* with a weak *isnad*.

اَللّٰهُمَّ رَبَّ السَّمٰوَاتِ السَّبْعِ وَمَا أَظْلَلْنَ ، وَرَبَّ الأَرْضِينَ السَّبْعِ وَمَا أَقْلَلْنَ ، وَرَبَّ الشَّيَاطِينَ وَمَا أَضْلَلْنَ ، وَرَبَّ الرِّيَاحِ وَمَا ذَرَيْنَ ، أَسْأَلُكَ خَيْرَ هَذِهِ الْقَرْيَةِ ، وَخَيْرَ أَهْلِهَا ، وَخَيْرَ مَا فِيهَا ، وَأَعُوذُ بِكَ مِنْ شَرِّهَا وَشَرِّ أَهْلِهَا ، وَشَرِّ مَا فِيهَا

"O Allah, Lord of the seven heavens and all that they shade, Lord of the seven lands and all that they support, Lord of the Shaytans and all that they lead astray, Lord of the winds and all that they carry, I ask You for the good of this village, the good of its people, and whatever good is in it; and I seek refuge with You from the mischief of this village, the mischief of its people, and whatever mischief is in it." (An-Nasa'i and others)

38. On stopping in a place during a journey

179. Khawlah bint Hakim ؓ said: I heard Allah's Messenger ﷺ say, "Whoever alights somewhere then says: ـ

أَعُوذُ بِكَلِمَاتِ اللّٰهِ التَّامَّاتِ مِنْ شَرِّ مَا خَلَقَ

'I seek refuge in Allah's perfect words from the mischief of what He has created,'

then nothing will harm him till he departs from that alighting-place of his." (Muslim)

180. ʿAbdullah ibn ʿUmar ؓ said: When Allah's Messenger ﷺ was travelling and night came on, he would say:

يَا أَرْضُ رَبِّي وَرَبُّكَ اللّٰهُ ، أَعُوذُ بِاللّٰهِ مِنْ شَرِّكَ وَشَرِّ مَا فِيكِ ، وَشَرِّ مَا خُلِقَ فِيكِ ، وَشَرِّ مَا يَدِبُّ عَلَيْكِ ، أَعُوذُ بِاللّٰهِ مِنْ أَسَدٍ وَأَسْوَدَ ، وَمِنَ الْحَيَّةِ وَالْعَقْرَبِ ، وَمِنْ سَاكِنِ الْبَلَدِ ، وَمِنْ وَالِدٍ وَمَا وَلَدَ

"O earth, my Lord and your Lord is Allah; I seek refuge in Allah from your mischief, the mischief of what you contain, the mischief of what has been created in you, and the mischief of what creeps upon you; I seek refuge in Allah from lions, from large black snakes, from other snakes, from scorpions, from the mischief of [jinn] which inhabit a settlement and from a parent and his offspring." (Abu Dawud)

39. On food and drink

Allah, exalted is He, says:

يَا أَيُّهَا الَّذِينَ آمَنُوا كُلُوا مِنْ طَيِّبَاتِ مَا رَزَقْنَاكُمْ وَاشْكُرُوا لِلَّهِ إِنْ كُنْتُمْ إِيَّاهُ تَعْبُدُونَ

"O you who believe! Eat of the good things with which We have provided you, and render thanks to Allah if it is [indeed] He whom you worship."

(Qur'an, al-Baqarah: 172)

181. ʿUmar ibn Abi Salamah ؓ said: Allah's Messenger ﷺ said to me, "My little son, mention Allah's name, eat with your right hand, and eat from what is next to you." (Bukhari, Muslim)

182. ʿA'ishah ؓ said: Allah's Messenger ﷺ said, "When one of you eats let him mention the name of Allah, exalted is He, at the beginning of it. If he forgets to mention Allah, exalted is He, at the beginning of it, he should say:

بِسْمِ اللَّهِ أَوَّلَهُ وَآخِرَهُ

'In the name of Allah at the beginning and at the end of it'."
(At-Tirmidhi transmitted it, saying, "A *hasan sahih hadith*.")

183. Umayyah ibn Makhshi ؓ said: The Messenger of Allah

ﷺ was seated and a man was eating, and he didn't mention Allah, exalted is He, until there was only a morsel left of his food. When he raised it to his mouth he said:

$$\text{بِسْمِ اللَّهِ أَوَّلَهُ وَآخِرَهُ}$$

"In the name of Allah at the beginning and at the end of it."

The Prophet ﷺ laughed and said, "The Shaytan kept eating along with him, but when he mentioned Allah's name, he vomited what was in his belly." (Abu Dawud and an-Nasa'i)

184. Abu Hurairah ؓ said: Allah's Messenger ﷺ never found fault with [any] food; if he had appetite for it, he ate it and if not, he left it. (Bukhari, Muslim)

185. Wahshi reported that the Companions of Allah's Messenger ﷺ said, "Messenger of Allah, we eat but do not feel satisfied." He said, "Perhaps you [eat] separately?" They said, "Yes." He ﷺ said, "Gather together for your food and mention Allah's name, you will be blessed in it." (Abu Dawud and Ibn Majah)

186. Anas ؓ said: Allah's Messenger ﷺ said, "Allah is pleased with a slave if he eats something and praises Him for it, and drinks something and praises Him for it." (Muslim)

187. Mu'adh ibn Anas ؓ said: Allah's Messenger ﷺ said, "Whoever eats food and says:

$$\text{الْحَمْدُ لِلَّهِ الَّذِي أَطْعَمَنِي هَذَا ، وَرَزَقَنِيهِ مِنْ غَيْرِ حَوْلٍ}$$
$$\text{مِنِّي وَلاَ قُوَّةٍ}$$

'Praise to Allah who has fed me this and provided me with it without power on my part nor strength,'

then all of his previous wrong actions will be forgiven." (At-Tirmidhi said, "A *hasan* hadith.")

188. Abu Saᶜid ﷺ related that when the Prophet ﷺ finished his food he would say:

الْحَمْدُ لِلَّهِ الَّذِي أَطْعَمَنَا ، وَسَقَانَا ، وَجَعَلَنَا مُسْلِمِينَ

✳ "Praise be to Allah who has given us food and drink and made us Muslims." (At-Tirmidhi, Abu Dawud)

189. A man who used to serve the Prophet ﷺ reported that he used to hear the Prophet ﷺ when he placed food before him, say:

بِسْمِ اللَّهِ

✳ "In the name of Allah,"
and when he finished eating he said:

اَللَّهُمَّ أَطْعَمْتَ ، وَأَسْقَيْتَ ، وَأَغْنَيْتَ ، وَأَقْنَيْتَ ، وَهَدَيْتَ ، وَأَحْيَيْتَ ، فَلَكَ الْحَمْدُ عَلَى مَا أَعْطَيْتَ

✳✳ "O Allah! You have given food and drink, and You have enriched and nourished, guided and given life. Praise belongs to You for what You have given." (An-Nasa'i and others)

190. Al-Bukhari transmitted from Abu Umamah ﷺ that when the tablecloth of the Prophet ﷺ was lifted up he said:

الْحَمْدُ لِلَّهِ كَثِيرًا طَيِّبًا مُبَارَكًا فِيهِ ، غَيْرَ مَكْفِيٍّ ، وَلَا مُوَدَّعٍ ، وَلَا مُسْتَغْنًى عَنْهُ رَبَّنَا

"Praise be to Allah abundantly and sincerely, of such a nature as is productive of blessing, is not insufficient, abandoned, or ignored, O our Lord."

40. On the guest and similar matters

191. ᶜAbdullah ibn Busr ؓ mentioned that: Allah's Messenger ﷺ visited my father and we presented him with some food and a mixture of dates, dried curd and clarified butter, some of which he ate. Then some dates were brought to him and he ate them, throwing away the stones between two fingers, joining the forefinger and the middle finger. He was then brought something to drink, which he drank and then gave to the one who was on his right. He [ᶜAbdullah ibn Busr] said: My father took hold of the bridle of his animal and said, "Supplicate Allah for us." So he said:

اَللَّهُمَّ بَارِكْ لَهُمْ فِيمَا رَزَقْتَهُمْ ، وَاغْفِرْ لَهُمْ ، وَارْحَمْهُمْ

"O Allah, bless them in that with which You have provided them, forgive them and show them mercy." (Muslim)

192. Anas ؓ related that the Prophet ﷺ came to visit Saᶜd ibn ᶜUbadah ؓ and he [Saᶜd] brought bread and olive oil, and he [the Prophet] ate. Then the Prophet ﷺ said:

أَفْطَرَ عِنْدَكُمُ الصَّائِمُونَ ، وَأَكَلَ طَعَامَكُمُ الأَبْرَارُ ، وَصَلَّتْ عَلَيْكُمُ الْمَلاَئِكَةُ

"May the ones who fast break their fast with you, and the pious eat your food, and the angels pray for blessing on you." (Abu Dawud and others)

193. Jabir ibn ᶜAbdullah ؓ said: Abu al-Haytham ibn at-Tayyihan prepared food for the Prophet ﷺ and he invited the Prophet ﷺ and his Companions. When they finished [eating], he said, "Reward your brother." They said, "Messenger of Allah, what is his reward?" He said, "If a man's house is entered, his food is eaten and his drink is drunk, and they supplicate [Allah] for him, that is his reward." (Abu Dawud.)

41. On greeting

194. ᶜAbdullah ibn ᶜAmr ﷺ said that a man asked Allah's Messenger ﷺ : "Which aspect of Islam is best?" He replied, "That you should provide food and greet both those you know and those you do not know." (Bukhari, Muslim)

195. Abu Hurairah ﷺ said: Allah's Messenger ﷺ said, "You will not enter the Garden till you believe, and you will not believe till you love one another. Let me guide you to something by doing which you will love one another. Spread the greeting of peace among you." (Muslim) *r. Good*

196. ᶜAmmar ibn Yasir ﷺ said, "There are three things which whoever unites them gathers together *iman*: to exact justice from yourself; to offer the greeting of peace to the world; and to spend in hardship."[1]

197. ᶜImran ibn Husayn said: A man came to the Prophet ﷺ and said:

السَّلَامُ عَلَيْكُمْ

"Peace be upon you,"
to which he responded and then the man sat down. The Prophet ﷺ said, "Ten." Another man came and said:

السَّلَامُ عَلَيْكُم وَرَحْمَةُ اللَّه

"Peace and Allah's mercy be upon you,"
to which he responded and then the man sat down. He said,

---

[1] Bukhari relates it like this as a *mawquf hadith*, i.e. one which stops short at the Companion, but Ibn Abi Shaybah and Ibn Hibban trace the text back to the Prophet ﷺ .

"Twenty." Another man came and said:

$$\text{السَّلَامُ عَلَيْكُم وَرَحْمَةُ اللَّهِ وَبَرَكَاتُهُ}$$

"*Peace and Allah's mercy and His blessings be upon you,*"
to which he responded and then the man sat down. He said,
"Thirty." (At-Tirmidhi transmitted it, saying, "A *hasan hadith*.")

198. Abu Umamah ﷜ said: Allah's Messenger ﷺ said, "Those who are nearest to Allah are they who are first to give [the greeting of] peace." (At-Tirmidhi transmitted it, saying, "A *hasan hadith*.")

199. Abu Dawud transmitted from ᶜAli ﷜ from the Prophet ﷺ: "It is enough for a group of people when they pass by, if one of them gives a greeting of peace, and it is enough for those who are sitting if one of them replies."

200. Anas ﷜ said: The Prophet ﷺ passed some children who were playing, and he gave them a greeting of peace. (A *sahih hadith*.)

201. Abu Hurairah ﷜ said: Allah's Messenger ﷺ said, "When one of you comes to an assembly of people he should give a greeting, and if he feels inclined to sit down, he should do so: then when he gets up, he should give a greeting, for the former [greeting] is not more of a duty than the latter." (At-Tirmidhi said, "A *hasan hadith*.")

42. On sneezing and yawning

202. Abu Hurairah ﷜ said that the Prophet ﷺ said, "Allah likes sneezing, but dislikes yawning. So when one of you sneezes and praises Allah, it is the duty of every Muslim who hears him to say:

$$\text{يَرْحَمُكَ اللَّهُ}$$

✻ *'May Allah have mercy on you!'*
But yawning comes only from the Shaytan, so when one of you yawns he should restrain it as much as possible, for when one of you yawns the Shaytan laughs at him." (Bukhari)

203. Abu Hurairah ﷺ also said that the Prophet ﷺ said, "When one of you sneezes he should say:

الْحَمْدُ لِلَّه

✻ *'Praise be to Allah!'*
and his brother, or his companion, should say to him,

يَرْحَمُكَ اللَّهُ

✻ *'May Allah have mercy on you!'*
When he says, 'May Allah have mercy on you!' to him he should reply:

يَهْدِيكُمُ اللَّهُ وَيُصْلِحُ بَالَكُمْ

✻ *'May Allah guide you and make good your state!'"* (Bukhari)
And in a version of Abu Dawud:

الْحَمْدُ لِلَّهِ عَلَى كُلِّ حَالٍ

✻ *"Praise be to Allah in every state!"*

204. Abu Musa al-Ashʿari ﷺ said: I heard Allah's Messenger ﷺ say, "When one of you sneezes and praises Allah, invoke a blessing on him, but if he does not praise Allah do not invoke a blessing on him." (Muslim)

43. On marriage

205. ʿAbdullah ibn Masʿud ﷺ said: Allah's Messenger ﷺ taught us the following *khutbat al-hajah* (*khutbah* of need):

الْحَمْدُ لِلَّه [نَحْمَدُهُ وَ] نَسْتَعِينُهُ ، وَنَسْتَغْفِرُهُ ، وَنَعُوذُ
بِاللَّه مِنْ شُرُورِ أَنْفُسِنَا ، وَسَيِّئَاتِ أَعْمَالِنَا ، مَنْ يَهْدِه
اللَّهُ فَلاَ مُضِلَّ لَهُ ، وَمَنْ يُضْلِلْ فَلاَ هَادِيَ لَهُ ، وَأَشْهَدُ أَنْ لاَ
إِلَهَ إِلاَّ اللَّهُ وَحْدَهُ لاَ شَرِيكَ لَهُ ، وَأَشْهَدُ أَنَّ مُحَمَّدًا عَبْدُهُ
وَرَسُولُهُ

*"Praise belongs to Allah, [we praise Him and] we seek His help!
We seek His forgiveness. We seek refuge with Allah from the evils
within ourselves, and the wrongs of our actions. Whomever Allah
guides there is none to lead astray; and whomever Allah leads
astray there is no guide for him. I witness that there is no god but
Allah alone without partner. And I witness that Muhammad is
His slave and His Prophet."*

and in another version there is this extra text:

أَرْسَلَهُ بِالْحَقِّ بَشِيرًا وَنَذِيرًا ، بَيْنَ يَدَيِ السَّاعَةِ ، مَنْ
يُطِعِ اللَّهَ وَرَسُولَهُ فَقَدْ رَشَدَ ، وَمَنْ يَعْصِهِمَا فَإِنَّهُ لاَ يَضُرُّ
إِلاَّ نَفْسَهُ ، وَلاَ يَضُرُّ اللَّهَ شَيْئًا

*"He sent him with the truth as a giver of good tidings and as a
warner before the coming of the Hour. Whoever obeys Allah
and His Messenger, has taken the right way. But whoever disobeys
them, harms no-one but himself, and does not harm Allah at
all.'"*

يَا أَيُّهَا النَّاسُ اتَّقُوا رَبَّكُمُ الَّذِي خَلَقَكُمْ مِنْ نَفْسٍ وَاحِدَةٍ
وَخَلَقَ مِنْهَا زَوْجَهَا وَبَثَّ مِنْهُمَا رِجَالاً كَثِيرًا وَنِسَاءً
وَاتَّقُوا اللَّهَ الَّذِي تَسَاءَلُونَ بِهِ وَالأَرْحَامَ إِنَّ اللَّهَ كَانَ عَلَيْكُمْ
رَقِيبًا

**"O Mankind, be fearfully careful of your Lord, who
created you from a single soul, and from it created its
mate and then has spread abroad from the two of them**

many men and women. Be careful of your duty towards Allah in Whom you claim [your rights] of one another, and toward the wombs [that bore you]. Surely Allah ever watches over you."

(Qur'an, an-Nisa': 1)

يَا أَيُّهَا الَّذِينَ آمَنُوا اتَّقُوا اللَّهَ حَقَّ تُقَاتِهِ وَلاَ تَمُوتُنَّ إِلاَّ وَأَنْتُمْ مُسْلِمُونَ

"O you who believe, be fearfully careful of Allah as He should be feared and do not die save as those who have surrendered [to Him]."

(Qur'an, Al Imran: 102)

يَا أَيُّهَا الَّذِينَ آمَنُوا اتَّقُوا اللَّهَ وَقُولُوا قَوْلاً سَدِيدًا يُصْلِحْ لَكُمْ أَعْمَالَكُمْ وَيَغْفِرْ لَكُمْ ذُنُوبَكُمْ وَمَنْ يُطِعِ اللَّهَ وَرَسُولَهُ فَقَدْ فَازَ فَوْزاً عَظِيمًا

"O you who believe, be fearfully careful of Allah and speak words straight to the point; He will set right your works for you and forgive you your wrong actions. Whoever obeys Allah and His Messenger has gained a great victory"

(Qur'an, al-Ahzab: 70-71)

(Abu Dawud, an-Nasa'i, Ibn Majah and at-Tirmidhi who said, "A *hasan hadith*.")

206. Abu Hurairah ﷺ said that when the Prophet ﷺ congratulated a man on his marriage he said:

بَارَكَ اللَّهُ لَكَ ، وَبَارَكَ عَلَيْكَ ، وَجَمَعَ بَيْنَكُمَا فِي خَيْرٍ

"*Allah bless you, and may He send blessings upon you, and may He unite you both in good.*" (At-Tirmidhi transmitted it, saying, "A *hasan sahih hadith*.")

207. ᶜAmr ibn Shuᶜaib related from his father, from his grandfather that the Prophet ﷺ said, "When any of you marries a woman, or buys a slave he should say:

$$\text{اَللّٰهُمَّ إِنِّي أَسْأَلُكَ خَيْرَهَا ، وَخَيْرَ مَا جَبَلْتَهَا عَلَيْهِ ، وَأَعُوذُ بِكَ مِنْ شَرِّهَا ، وَشَرِّ مَا جَبَلْتَهَا عَلَيْهِ}$$

'O Allah, I ask You for the good in her and the good in the disposition You have given her, and I seek refuge in You from the mischief in her and from the mischief in the disposition You have given her.'

When he buys a camel he should take hold of the top of its hump and say the same kind of thing." (Abu Dawud and Ibn Majah)

208. Ibn ᶜAbbas ﷜ narrated Allah's Messenger ﷺ as saying, "If any of you who means to have intercourse with his wife says:

$$\text{بِسْمِ اللّٰهِ ، اَللّٰهُمَّ جَنِّبْنَا الشَّيْطَانَ وَجَنِّبِ الشَّيْطَانَ مَا رَزَقْتَنَا}$$

"In the name of Allah. O Allah, keep us away from the Shaytan and keep the Shaytan away from what You provide us,"

should it be decreed that a child be born to them thereby, no Shaytan will ever harm it." (Bukhari, Muslim)

44. On birth Fatimah's

209. It is mentioned that when the time of Fatimah's delivery came ﷜ the Messenger of Allah ﷺ told Umm Salamah and Zaynab bint Jahsh to recite near her the *Ayat al-Kursi* and:

$$\text{إِنَّ رَبَّكُمُ اللّٰهُ الَّذِي خَلَقَ السَّمٰوَاتِ وَالْأَرْضَ فِي سِتَّةِ أَيَّامٍ ثُمَّ اسْتَوَى عَلَى الْعَرْشِ ، يُغْشِي اللَّيْلَ النَّهَارَ يَطْلُبُهُ}$$

94

حَثِيثاً وَالشَّمْسَ وَالْقَمَرَ وَالنُّجُومَ مُسَخَّرَاتٍ بِأَمْرِهِ ، أَلَا
لَهُ الْخَلْقُ وَالأَمْرُ ، تَبَارَكَ اللَّهُ رَبُّ الْعَالَمِينَ

"Truly, your Lord is Allah who created the heavens and the earth in six days, then He mounted the Throne. He covers the night with the day, which is in haste to follow it, and has made the sun and moon and the stars subservient by His command. His truly is all creation and command. Blessed be Allah, the Lord of the Worlds." (Qur'an, al-A'raf: 54)

and Surah Yunus *ayah* 3, and they should pray for her protection by reciting *Al-Mu'awwidhatain*.

210. Abu Rafi' ﷺ said: I saw the Prophet ﷺ giving the *adhan* of the prayer in the ear of Hasan ibn 'Ali when Fatimah ﷺ gave birth to him. (At-Tirmidhi said, "A *hasan* hadith.")

211. And it is mentioned of Husain ibn 'Ali ﷺ that he said: The Messenger of Allah ﷺ said, "Whoever has a child born to him and he gives the *adhan* in his right ear and recites the *iqamah* in his left ear, then Umm as-Sibyan will not harm him."[1]

212. 'A'ishah ﷺ said: New born children were brought to the Messenger of Allah ﷺ and he would pray for blessings for them and chew a date and put it on the child's palate. (Abu Dawud)

213. 'Amr ibn Shu'aib narrated from his father, from his grandfather from the Prophet ﷺ that he ordered that a newborn child should be given a name on its seventh day, and it should be cleansed, and [he ordered] for its *aqiqah* (that its hair should be shaved and

---

[1] Ibn as-Sunni transmitted it with an *isnad* which has two among its narrators who were accused of fabrication while the third narrator is weak. Imam al-Baihaqi transmitted it from al-Hasan ibn 'Ali, while here in this book it is from al-Husain ibn 'Ali, and like this Imam an-Nawawi mentioned it in his book, *Al-Adhkar*.

a sheep or goat sacrificed for him or her). (At-Tirmidhi said, "A *hasan hadith*.")

214. The Prophet ﷺ named his son Ibrahim, and he named Ibrahim the son of Abu Musa, ᶜAbdullah the son of Abi Talhah, and Mundhir the son of Abu Usayd, soon after their births.

215. Abu ad-Darda' ؓ said: Allah's Messenger ﷺ said, "You will be called on the Day of Resurrection by your names and your fathers' names, so give yourselves good names." (Abu Dawud)

216. Muslim mentioned in his *sahih* that ᶜAbdullah ibn ᶜUmar ؓ said: Allah's Messenger ﷺ said, "The most beloved of your names to Allah are ᶜAbdullah and ᶜAbd ar-Rahman." (Muslim)

217. Abu Wahb al-Jushami ؓ said: Allah's Messenger ﷺ said, "Call yourselves by the names of the prophets. The most beloved of your names to Allah are ᶜAbdullah and ᶜAbd ar-Rahman, the truest are Harith (a collector of property) and Hammam (worrier), and the ugliest are Harb (war) and Murrah (bitterness)." (Abu Dawud and an-Nasa'i)

218. The Prophet ﷺ changed unpleasant names to good names. Zaynab was [originally] named Barrah (obedience). It was said, "She declares herself pure." So he re-named her Zaynab. He disliked that it should be said, "He has come away from obedience (Barrah)." (Muslim)

He said to a man, "What is your name?" He said, "Hazan (rugged)." He said, "Rather you are Sahl (smooth, or at ease)." He changed the name of ᶜAsiyah (disobedient) and called her Jamilah (beautiful). He asked a man, "What is your name?" He said, "Asram (one cut off)." He said, "Rather you are Zurᶜah (a seed, or land in which to sow)." He named Harb (war) Silm (peace). He named al-Mudtajiʿ (asleep) al-Munbaʿith (awake). A land known as ʿAfrah (barren) he named Khadirah (green, verdant). Shiʿb ad-Dalalah (the valley of misguidance) he named Shiʿb al-Huda (the valley of guidance). Banu az-Zinyah (children, or tribe of adultery) he named Banu ar-Rashdah (children, or tribe of valid marriage).

45. On cockcrows, braying, and barking

219. Abu Hurairah مُنْهُ mentioned of the Prophet صلى الله عليه وسلم that he said, "When you hear an ass braying then seek refuge in Allah from the Shaytan, for it has seen a shaytan; but when you hear the cocks crowing ask Allah for some of His grace, for they have seen an angel." (Bukhari, Muslim)

220. Jabir مُنْهُ said: Allah's Messenger صلى الله عليه وسلم said, "When you hear the barking of dogs and the braying of asses at night seek refuge in Allah from them, for they see what you do not see." (Abu Dawud)

46. On fire

221. It is mentioned from ʿAmr ibn Shuʿaib from his father, from his grandfather that he said: The Messenger of Allah صلى الله عليه وسلم said, "When you see fire say اَللَّهُ أَكْبَرُ 'Allah is Greater', for the *takbir* will extinguish it."[1]

47. On a gathering

222. Abu Hurairah مُنْهُ said: Allah's Messenger صلى الله عليه وسلم said, "Whoever sits in an assembly where there is much clamour and says before getting up to leave:

---

[1] A *daʿif hadith* as the author hinted. ʿUqayli transmitted it in *ad-duʿafa*, Ibn ʿAdi in *al-kamil* and Ibn as-Sunni in his book *ʿamal al-yawm wallaylah* from a very weak line of narrators.

سُبْحَانَكَ اللَّهُمَّ وَبِحَمْدِكَ ، أَشْهَدُ أَنْ لاَ إِلَهَ إِلاَّ أَنْتَ ،
أَسْتَغْفِرُكَ وَأَتُوبُ إِلَيْكَ

*'Glory be to You, O Allah and [I begin] with praise of You; I
witness that there is no god but You; I ask Your forgiveness and
turn to You in repentance,'*

Allah will cover over for him what took place in that assembly of
his." (At-Tirmidhi said, "A *hasan sahih hadith*.")

223. In another *hadith*, "If it was a good gathering, it will be as a
seal for it and if it is a gathering of all sorts, it will be an expiation."

224. Abu Hurairah ﷺ said: The Messenger of Allah ﷺ said,
"People who get up from an assembly in which they did not
remember Allah, exalted is He, will be just as if they had got up
from an ass's corpse, and it will be a cause of grief to them." (Abu
Dawud and others)

225. Ibn ʿUmar ﷺ said: Allah's Messenger ﷺ seldom got up
to leave an assembly without using these supplications for his
companions:

اَللَّهُمَّ اقْسِمْ لَنَا مِنْ خَشْيَتِكَ مَا تَحُولُ بِهِ بَيْنَنَا وَبَيْنَ
مَعَاصِيكَ ، وَمِنْ طَاعَتِكَ مَا تُبَلِّغُنَا بِهِ جَنَّتَكَ ، وَمِنَ الْيَقِينِ
مَا تُهَوِّنُ بِهِ عَلَيْنَا مَصَائِبَ الدُّنْيَا ، اَللَّهُمَّ مَتِّعْنَا
بِأَسْمَاعِنَا ، وَأَبْصَارِنَا ، وَقُوَّتِنَا مَا أَحْيَيْتَنَا ، وَاجْعَلْهُ
الْوَارِثَ مِنَّا ، وَاجْعَلْ ثَأْرَنَا عَلَى مَنْ ظَلَمَنَا ، وَانْصُرْنَا
عَلَى مَنْ عَادَانَا ، وَلاَ تَجْعَلْ مُصِيبَتَنَا فِي دِينِنَا ، وَلاَ
تَجْعَلِ الدُّنْيَا أَكْبَرَ هَمِّنَا ، وَلاَ مَبْلَغَ عِلْمِنَا ، وَلاَ تُسَلِّطْ
عَلَيْنَا مَنْ لاَ يَرْحَمُنَا

"O Allah, apportion to us such fear of You as will come between

98

us and acts of disobedience to You, and such obedience to You by which You will bring us to Your Garden, and such certainty by which you will make the calamities of this world seem insignificant to us; O Allah, let us enjoy our hearing, our sight and our power as long as You grant us life, and do the same for those who inherit from us; grant us revenge on those who have wronged us and help us against those who are hostile to us; don't put our calamity in our din, and do not make the world our greatest care or the full extent of our knowledge, and do not put in authority over us one who shows us no mercy." (At-Tirmidhi transmitted it, saying, "A hasan hadith.")

48. On anger

Allah, exalted is He, says:

وَإِمَّا يَنْزَغَنَّكَ مِنَ الشَّيْطَانِ نَزْغٌ فَاسْتَعِذْ بِاللَّهِ إِنَّهُ هُوَ السَّمِيعُ الْعَلِيمُ

'And if an incitement from the Shaytan reaches you then seek refuge in Allah. Truly, He is the Hearer, the Knower.'"
(Qur'an, Fussilat: 36)

226. Sulayman ibn Surad ﷺ said: I was sitting with the Messenger of Allah ﷺ and two men reviled one another, and the face of one of them started getting red and his jugular vein stuck out. The Messenger of Allah ﷺ said, "I know a phrase which if he repeated it then his angry feelings would leave him. If he says:

أَعُوذُ بِاللَّهِ مِنَ الشَّيْطَانِ الرَّجِيمِ

'I seek refuge in Allah from the accursed Shaytan,'
then that which he finds in himself would leave him." (Bukhari, Muslim)

227. ʿAtiyyah ibn ʿUrwah said: Allah's Messenger ﷺ said, "Anger

is from the Shaytan, and the Shaytan is created of fire, and fire is only extinguished with water; so when one of you becomes angry he should perform *wudu.*" (Abu Dawud)

49. On seeing afflicted people

228. Abu Hurairah ☺ reported the Prophet ﷺ as saying, "Whoever sees someone who is suffering affliction and says:

$$ اَلْحَمْدُ لِلَّهِ الَّذِي عَافَانِي مِمَّا ابْتَلَاكَ اللَّهُ بِهِ ، وَفَضَّلَنِي عَلَى كَثِيرٍ مِمَّنْ خَلَقَ تَفْضِيلاً $$

'Praise be to Allah who has kept me free from that which He has tested you with, and has shown me favour above many whom He has created,'

that affliction will not smite him." (At-Tirmidhi said, "A *hasan hadith.*")

50. On entering the market place

229. ʿUmar ibn al-Khattab ☺ reported that Allah's Messenger ﷺ said, "Whoever enters the market and says:

$$ لَا إِلَهَ إِلاَّ اللَّهُ وَحْدَهُ لَا شَرِيكَ لَهُ ، لَهُ الْمُلْكُ ، وَلَهُ الْحَمْدُ ، يُحْيِي وَيُمِيتُ ، وَهُوَ حَيٌّ لَا يَمُوتُ ، بِيَدِهِ الْخَيْرُ ، وَهُوَ عَلَى كُلِّ شَيْءٍ قَدِيرٌ $$

'There is no god but Allah alone without partner; His is the dominion, and His the praise, He gives life and causes death, while He is Living and does not die; in His hand is the good, and He has power over all things,'

Allah will record for him a million good deeds, obliterate from him a million wrong actions, and raise him a million degrees." (At-Tirmidhi)

230. Buraidah ☙ said: Allah's Messenger ☙ said, when he went out to go to the market:

بِسْمِ اللَّهِ ، اَللَّهُمَّ إِنِّي أَسْأَلُكَ [مِنْ] خَيْرِ هَذِهِ السُّوقِ ، وَخَيْرِ مَا فِيهَا ، وَأَعُوذُ بِكَ مِنْ شَرِّهَا ، وَشَرَّ مَا فِيهَا ، اَللَّهُمَّ إِنِّي أَعُوذُ بِكَ أَنْ أُصِيبَ فِيهَا يَمِينًا فَاجِرَةً ، أَوْ صَفْقَةً خَاسِرَةً

"In the name of Allah. O Allah, I ask You for the good of this market and the good of what is in it, and I seek refuge with You from its mischief and the mischief of what is in it. O Allah, I seek refuge in You lest I receive a deceitful oath or a bad bargain in it."

(Its *isnad* is better than the previous one.)

51. When looking in the mirror

231. It is mentioned from Anas ☙ that he said: When Allah's Messenger ☙ looked [at his face] in the mirror he said:

الْحَمْدُ للَّهِ الَّذِي سَوَّى خَلْقِي فَعَدَّلَهُ ، وَكَرَّمَ صُورَةَ وَجْهِي فَحَسَّنَهَا ، وَجَعَلَنِي مِنَ الْمُسْلِمِينَ

"Praise belongs to Allah who has shaped my physical appearance and balanced it, and who has made the form of my face good, and He made me one of the Muslims."

232. ʿAli ☙ related that when the Prophet ☙ saw his face in the mirror he said:

الْحَمْدُ للَّهِ ، اَللَّهُمَّ كَمَا حَسَّنْتَ خَلْقِي فَحَسِّنْ خُلُقِي

"Praise be to Allah, O Allah, just as You made my physical appearance good, make my character good."[1]

---

[1] This *hadith* and No. 231 are both *daʿif*. Ibn as-Sunni and others have

101

52. On cupping (a medical treatment)

233. ʿAli said: The Messenger of Allah said, "Whoever recites *Ayat al-Kursi* while being cupped, then his cupping will be of benefit."

53. On buzzing in the ear

234. Abu Rafiʿ said: The Messenger of Allah said, "If one of you feels a humming in his ear, he should remember me and pray for blessings for me and should say:

$$\text{ذَكَرَ اللَّهُ بِخَيْرٍ مَنْ ذَكَرَنِي}$$

 'May Allah remember with good the one who remembers me'."[1]

54. On numbness of the feet

235. Haytham ibn Hanash said: We were with ʿAbdullah ibn ʿUmar. His foot became numb. A man said to him, "Remember the one whom you love most." He said, "Muhammad." and it was as if he had been set free from a hobbling cord.

236. Mujahid said: A man's foot was numb and he was sitting with Ibn ʿAbbas. Ibn ʿAbbas said to him, "Remember the person whom you love most." He said, "Muhammad" and his numbness was cured.

55. On the animal when it stumbles

237. Abu al-Malih reported on the authority of a man: I was riding on

---

transmitted them, but it is authentically narrated that the Prophet prayed with the latter *duʿa*, without the description of looking into the mirror.

[1] Ibn as-Sunni and at-Tabarani in three of his books. It is very weak.

a mount behind the Prophet ﷺ. It stumbled.
Thereupon I said, "May the Shaytan perish!"
He ﷺ said, "Do not say, 'May the Shaytan perish!' for if you say
that, he will swell so much [with pride] that he will be like a house,
and he will say, 'By my power!' But say:

$$\text{بِسْمِ اللَّه}$$

* 'In the name of Allah',
for when you say that, he will diminish so much until he is like a
fly." (Abu Dawud)

56. On one who gives a gift and the recipient prays for him

238. ʿAʾishah ﷺ said: Someone sent a ewe to the Prophet ﷺ
as a gift. He said, "Distribute it." ʿAʾishah used to ask the servant
when she returned, "What did they say?" The servant said, "They
said:

$$\text{بَارَكَ اللَّهُ فِيكُمْ}$$

* 'May Allah bless you.'"
ʿAʾishah said:

$$\text{وَفِيهِمْ بَارَكَ اللَّهُ}$$

* "'And them may Allah bless.'
We respond to them with the like of what they answered, and so
our reward will remain with us."
"It reached us that when she [ʿAʾishah] gave sadaqah she would
do the same."

57. On what one says when a harm is removed from him

239. It is related from Abu Ayyub al-Ansari ﷺ that he removed
something unclean from the beard of the Messenger of Allah ﷺ.

Allah's Messenger ﷺ said:

مَسَحَ اللَّهُ عَنْكَ يَا أَبَا أَيُّوبَ مَا تَكْرَهُ

✳ *"May Allah remove from you, O Abu Ayyub, that which you dislike."*
One variant is

لاَ يَكُنْ بِكَ السُّوءُ يَا أَبَا أَيُّوبَ

✳ *"May no harm be with you, O Abu Ayyub."*[1]

240. It is related that ʿUmar ﷺ took something from a man's beard or from his head, and the man said, "May Allah avert mischief from you." ʿUmar ﷺ said, "Allah has averted mischief from us since we became Muslims, but when something [unclean or unpleasant] is taken from you say:

أَخَذَتْ يَدَاكَ خَيْرًا

✳ *"May your two hands take good."*[2]

58. Seeing the first fruits of the season

241. Abu Hurairah ﷺ said, "When people saw the first fruits [of the season], they brought them to the Messenger of Allah ﷺ. When the Messenger of Allah ﷺ took them he said:

اَللَّهُمَّ بَارِكْ لَنَا فِي ثَمَـرِنَا ، وَبَارِكْ لَنَا فِي مَـدِينَتِنَا ، وَبَارِكْ لَنَا فِي صَاعِنَا ، وَبَارِكْ لَنَا فِي مُدِّنَا

'O Allah! Bless us in our fruits. Bless us in our Madinah. Bless us in our saʿ and bless us in our mudd.'
Then he gave them to the smallest child there." (Muslim)[3]

---

[1] A *daʿif hadith*. Ibn as-Sunni transmitted both versions.

[2] It has a good *isnad*; Ibn as-Sunni transmitted it.

[3] The *mudd* is what the two cupped hands can hold, e.g. of grains, pulses, dates, etc. A *mudd* is one quarter of a *saʿ* which is equal in metric weight to

59. Admiring something and fear of the evil eye

Allah, exalted is He, says:

وَلَوْ لاَ إِذْ دَخَلْتَ جَنَّتَكَ قُلْتَ مَا شَاءَ اللَّهُ لاَ قُوَّةَ إِلاَّ بِاللَّه

"If only, when you entered your garden, you had said, 'That which Allah wills [will come to pass]! There is no strength save in Allah.'"

(Qur'an, al-Kahf: 39)

242. The Prophet ﷺ said, "The [evil] eye is a reality. If anything could overcome the decree, the [evil] eye would overcome it." (A *sahih hadith*)

243. It is mentioned that the Prophet ﷺ said, "If one of you sees something he admires in his self or his property, he should pray for blessings on himself, because the [evil] eye is a reality."[1]

244. It is mentioned that the Prophet ﷺ said, "Whoever of you sees something he admires should say:

مَا شَاءَ اللَّهُ لاَ قُوَّةَ إِلاَّ بِاللَّه

'That which Allah wills [will come to pass]! There is no strength save in Allah.'"

(Qur'an, al-Kahf: 39)[2]

245. It is mentioned from the Prophet ﷺ that when he feared that his eye might affect something he would say:

اَللَّهُمَّ بَارِكْ فِيهِ وَلاَ تَضُرَّهُ

"O Allah bless it and do not harm it."[3]

3.17kg in the case of grains, for example.

[1] A *sahih hadith* transmitted by Ibn as-Sunni

[2] A *hadith* whose *isnad* is weak; Ibn as-Sunni transmitted it.

246. Abu Saⁿid ﷺ said: The Messenger ﷺ used to seek refuge from the Jinn and from the [evil] eye of the human until *al-Muⁿawwidhatain* were revealed. When they were revealed, he took them and left everything else. (At-Tirmidhi said, "A *hasan hadith*.")

60. On good and bad omens

247. The Prophet ﷺ said, "There is no contagion and no evil omen, and the truest of them is the good omen." They asked, "What is a good omen." He replied, "A good word which a man hears."

248. The Messenger of Allah ﷺ was pleased with good omens.

249. For example as it happened on the journey of the Hijrah; a man met them and he (the Prophet) said, "What is your name?" The man said, "Buraidah." He (the Prophet) said, "Our matter has become easy (بَرَدَ)."

250. He ﷺ said, "I saw in my sleep as if I was in the house of ⁿUqbah ibn Rafiⁿ. We were brought some of the fresh dates of Ibn Tab. I interpreted it as meaning eminence (الرِّفْعَة) for us in this world, the ultimate end (الْعَاقِبَة) will be for us in the hereafter, and that our *din* is good (طَاب lit: fragrant)."

251. As for bad omens, Muⁿawiyyah ibn al-Hakam ﷺ said: I said, "Messenger of Allah, among us there are men who draw bad omens." He said, "That is a thing which you find in your breasts, so don't let it divert you." ·

(All of these *ahadith* are in the *sahih* collections.)

---

[3] A *hadith* whose *isnad* is weak as the author hinted; Ibn as-Sunni transmitted it.

252. ʿUrwah ibn ʿAmir said: Allah's Messenger ﷺ was asked about omens and he said, "The truest of them is the good omen, and it should not turn a Muslim back. If you see anything you dislike then say:

اَللَّهُمَّ لاَ يَأْتِي بِالْحَسَنَاتِ إِلاَّ أَنْتَ ، وَلاَ يَذْهَبُ بِالسَّيِّئَاتِ إِلاَّ أَنْتَ ، وَلاَ حَوْلَ وَلاَ قُوَّةَ إِلاَّ بِاللَّهِ

'O Allah, no one brings good things but You, no-one takes away bad things but You, and there is no might or strength but by Allah.'" [1]

61. On the public bath

253. Abu Hurairah ﷺ said, "What an excellent house is the Hammam (public bath)[2] which the Muslim enters. When he enters it, he asks Allah for the Garden and seeks refuge with Him from the Fire."[3]

---

[1] Abu Dawud transmitted it. There is some weakness in the isnad.

[2] On the condition that one observes the rules of shariʿah on modesty and privacy.

[3] It is daʿif; Ibn as-Sunni transmitted it.

Transliteration of Arabic Names and Terms

Allāh ﷻ
Muḥammad ﷺ
'Abdullāh
'Abdullāh ibn 'Abbās
'Abdullāh ibn 'Amr
'Abdullāh ibn Busr
'Abdullāh ibn Ghannām
'Abdullāh ibn Khubayb
'Abdullāh ibn Mas'ūd
'Abdullāh ibn 'Umar
'Abdullāh ibn az-Zubayr
Abū Ayyūb al-Anṣārī
Abū Bakrah
Abū Bakr aṣ-Ṣiddīq
Abū ad-Dardā'
Abū Dāwūd
Abū al-Haytham ibn at Tayyihān
Abū Ḥumaid
Abū Hurayrah
Abu'l 'Abbās
Abu'l-Malīḥ
Abū Mālik al-Ash'arī
Abū Mas'ūd
Abū Mūsā al-Ash'arī
Abū Naṣr
Abū Qatādah ibn ar-Rabī'

Abū Rāfi'
Abū Sa'īd
Abū Sa'īd al-Khudrī
Abū Salamāh ibn 'Abd
  ar-Raḥmān
Abū Ṣāliḥ
Abū Ṭalḥah
Abū Umāmah
Abū Usayd
Abū Wahb al-Jushamī
Abū Ya'lā al-Mawṣilī
Abū Zumail
Adhān
'Afrah
Aḥad
Aḥādīth
Aḥmad
Al-Aḥzāb
'Ā'ishah
'Alī ibn Abī Ṭalib
'Alī ibn Rabī'ah
'Ālij
Allāhu Akbar
Āmīn
Amīr al-Mu'minīn
'Ammār ibn Yāsir

'Amr ibn 'Abasah
'Amr ibn Shu'aib
Al-An'ām
Anas ibn Mālik
Al-Anbiyā'
Al-Anfāl
Al-A'rāf
'Āṣiyah
Asmā' bint 'Umays
'Aṣr
Aṣram
'Aṭā' ibn as-Sā'ib
'Aṭiyyah ibn 'Urwah
'Awf ibn Mālik
Āyah
Āyāt
Āyat-al-Kursī
al-Baihaqī
Banū Hārithah
Banū ar-Rashdah
Banū az-Zinyah
Al-Barā' ibn 'Āzib
Bilāl
Bukhārī
Buraidah
Ad-Dārimī
Dīn
Dhu'n-Nūn (Yūnus)
Du'ā'
al-Fātiḥah
Fāṭimah
Fuṣṣilat
Ghāfir
Gharīb
al-Ḥadīd

Ḥadīth
Ḥāfiẓ Ibn Ḥajar
Ḥafṣah, Umm al-Mu'minīn
Ḥajj
al-Ḥākim
Ḥanīf
Ḥarb
Ḥasan ibn 'Alī
Haytham ibn Ḥanash
Ḥazn
Hūd
Ḥudaybiyyah
Ḥudhayfah
Ḥusain ibn 'Alī
'Ibādah
Iblīs
Ibn 'Abbās
Ibn Abī Mulaykah
Ibn Abī Shaybah
Ibn 'Adī
Ibn Ḥibbān
Ibn Mājah
Ibn Mas'ūd
Ibn as-Sunnī
Ibrāhīm
'Īd
Imām Mālik
Īmān
Āl 'Imrān
'Imrān ibn Ḥuṣayn
Iqāmah
Isḥāq
Islām
Ismā'īl
Isnād

Al-Isrā'
Isrāfīl
Istighfār
Istikhārah
Istisqā'
Jābir ibn 'Abdullāh
Jamīlah
Jibrīl
Jihād
Jubair ibn Muṭ'im
Juwairiyah
Khadījah
Khālid ibn al-Walīd
Khalīfah
Khawlah bint Ḥakīm
Khuṭbat al-Ḥājah
Kitāb al-Adhkār
Madīnah
Mālik
Mawqūf
Mīkā'īl
Mu'adhdhin
Mu'ādh ibn Anas
Mu'ādh ibn Jabal
Mu'āwiyah ibn al-Ḥakam
al-Mu'awwidhatain
al-Muḍṭaji'
Mufarridūn
Al-Mughīrah ibn Shu'bah
Muhājirūn
Muḥyiddīn Abū Zakariyyā Yaḥyā
   ibn Sharaf an-Nawawī
Mujāhid
al-Mumba'ith
al-Mu'minūn

Al-Munāfiqūn
Muṣallā
al-Muzzammil
Naḍr ibn Shumail
An-Nasā'ī
Nāṣiruddīn al-Albānī
An-Nisā'
An-Nūr
Qāf
Qul A'ūdhu Bi Rabbil Falaq
Qul A'ūdhu Bi Rabbin Nās
Qur'ān
Rak'ah
Rifā'ah ibn Rāfi'
Rukū'
Ar-Rūm
Ṣā'
Sa'd ibn Abī Waqqāṣ
Sa'd ibn 'Ubādah
Ṣadaqah
Ṣaḥīḥ
Sahl ibn Sa'd
Ṣalāh
Sālim
Samurah ibn Jundub
Shaddād ibn Aws
Shamsuddīn
Sharī'ah
Shayṭān
Shi'b aḍ-Ḍalālah
Shi'b al-Hudā
Ṣiffīn
Su'ād
Sufyān ibn 'Uyaynah
Suhail ibn 'Abī Ṣāliḥ

Sulaymān ibn Ṣurad
Sūrah
Aṭ-Ṭabarānī
Tahajjud
Tahlīl
Taḥmīd
Takbīr
Ṭalq ibn Ḥabīb
Taqiyyuddīn
Taqwā
Tasbīḥ
Tashahhud
Taslīm
Tawfīq
Thawbān
At-Tirmidhī
Aṭ-Ṭūr
'Ubādah ibn aṣ-Ṣāmit
'Umar ibn Abī Salamah
'Umar ibn al-Khaṭṭāb

Umayyah ibn Makhshī
Umm al-Mu'minīn
Umm Salamah
Umm aṣ-Ṣibyān
'Umrah
'Uqbah ibn 'Āmir
'Uqbah ibn Rāfi'
'Urwah ibn 'Āmir
'Uthmān ibn 'Affān
'Uthmān ibn Abi'l-'Āṣ
Waḥshī
Wakī'
Wasīlah
Wuḍū'
Yūnus ibn 'Ubaid
Zakāh
Zayd ibn Aslam
Zayd ibn Khālid al-Juhanī
Zaynab bint Jaḥsh
Zur'ah